The Meaning of Idealism

The Metaphysics of Genus and Countenance

PAVEL FLORENSKY

THE
MEANING
OF
IDEALISM

The Metaphysics of
Genus and Countenance

Translated & Edited by
BORIS JAKIM

First published in the USA
by Semantron Press
an imprint of Angelico Press
© Boris Jakim 2020

For information, address:
Angelico Press, Ltd.
169 Monitor St., Brooklyn, NY 11222
www.angelicopress.com

978-1-62138-530-1 pbk
978-1-62138-635-3 cloth
978-1-62138-531-8 ebook

Cover design: Michael Schrauzer
Cover image: Group IX/SUW,
The Swan, No. 13, by Hilma af Klint

CONTENTS

Translator's Note 1

1 What is Platonism? 3

2 Symbols of Platonism 7

3 Idealism and the Theory of Knowledge 11

4 Plotinus and Neoplatonism 15

5 Porphyry's Conception 19

6 The One and the Many 23

7 Ideals as an Embodiment of Life: Rodin 33

8 The Esthetic Problem of the Portrait 39

9 Hinton and the Higher Consciousness 45

10 Picasso 49

11 Four-Dimensional Perception 53

12 The Meaning of Genus 65

13 Genus and Species 69

14 Idea and Countenance 79

15 The Fundamental Aspirations of Idealism 87

16 *Genesis*, *Genitura*, and *Gandhara* 91

Translator's Note

PAVEL FLORENSKY'S treatment of Platonism in the present work is one of the most important treatises on this subject ever written. The great scholar of antiquity, Aleksei Losev, called *The Meaning of Idealism* the most profound work on Platonism and Idealism produced in the 20th century. The work is a journey—from Plato and Aristotle to Neoplatonism, from Neoplatonism to Medieval theories, from Medieval theories to Orthodox spirituality, from Orthodox spirituality to Vedic mysticism, from Vedic mysticism to astrology, from astrology to modern science—including relativity, the mathematical theory of invariants, and the multidimensional universe. In this journey, Florensky corroborates his theories with etymological discussions and analyses of modern art, including the works of Rodin and Picasso.

The new thing Florensky introduces in his interpretation of idealism is the doctrine of genus and spiritual countenance (*lik* in Russian, related to *litso*, face, and *lichnost*, person). Florensky links his understanding of the Platonic idea with images of the ancient gods and their use in the ancient mysteries. He writes: "The enigmatic kernel of Platonism is mystery; for the goal of initiation was identical to the goal of philosophy: to develop the capacity for mystical contemplation and directly to see *mistika theamata* (mystical visions)."

Florensky's conception is mythological, and the unprecedented thing he discovers in Platonism is the symbolic-magical nature of myth. Florensky's method presupposes a purely intuitive penetration into the essence of things, into genus and species—a penetration that is not abstract but is linked with a concrete embodiment of ideas accessible to all the senses, especially vision. Thus the Russian philosopher N. O. Lossky underscores the great value of Florensky's interpretation of Platonic ideas, not as abstract concepts, but as living concrete persons (countenances).

The Meaning of Idealism was conceived as part of the "watersheds of thought" project, Florensky's multivolume study of "anthropodicy," where the ways of man are justified before God.

Originally delivered as a series of lectures at the Moscow Religious Academy, the essay was first published in 1915. The present translation uses the text given in the *Collected Works of Pavel Florensky*, volume 3(2), ed. Igumen Andronik (A. S. Trubachev), Moscow, 1999. Some notes have been shortened or eliminated.

BORIS JAKIM
March 2020

1

What is
Platonism?

EVERYONE IS FAMILIAR with the term "Platonism." Equally
familiar is the fact that what this name designates is not only a
historical phenomenon but also an abiding expression of the
inner life of man. However, in both its historical and its spiritual
aspect, Platonism is an extremely complex phenomenon—so
complex that, to the present day, historians of thought have not
been able to clarify it fully. Platonism is a variegated wreath: the
beloved sweet-smelling grasses of our native meadows are intertwined with the mysterious orchids of the East; the blooms of
ancient Athens merge with the sacred lotuses of the Nile. Who
would be bold enough to undertake the infinitely daunting task
of giving a precise definition of Platonism? And if you ask me
"What is Platonism?"—I too must answer "Alas, I do not
know." And I am not alone. This unavoidable *non liquet* (lack of
clarity) of mine is something that afflicts all historians of thought
and culture. "At the present time," one such historian remarks,
"we have no choice but to agree with the Platonic philosopher
Origen that no one fully understands Plato."[1]

We know that Platonism is a powerful spiritual movement. We
know that at least half of all philosophy (the most beautiful half)

1. A.I. Giliarov, *Survey of Works on the History of Thought and Culture* (for
1892–1896), Kiev, 1896, 12.

is associated with the name Plato. Even a staunch opponent of Platonism admits "that all the domains that are subsumed under the name idealism—realism in logic, apriorism, nativism, or rationalism in the theory of knowledge, and spiritualism and teleology in ontology—have the same source: namely the thinker who, though he was not the first to attribute a scientific sense to the term 'idea,' was the first to impart to it a universally historical character. This thinker was Plato."[2]

We know that the greater part of everything that is magnificent in poetry is a reflection of the rays streaming from Plato. We know that the languages of all nations are suffused with Platonic terms and Platonic concepts. We know that Platonism has shed light on many different national religions and different ways of understanding the meaning of life. We know that virtually all the powerful currents in philosophy have their source in Platonism. We know that Platonism has served as a mighty stimulus for religious thought—not only in paganism, but also in Christianity; not only in Christianity, but also in Islam and Judaism. Platonism is the worldview that conforms most closely to religion as such, and its terminology expresses better than any other the religious life of man. But while being the natural philosophy of every religion, Platonism has a particular kinship with that religion before which all the others just barely retain the name "religion." In short, we know that Platonism is a powerful (one can even say, the most powerful) stimulus of cultural life.

But the question What is Platonism? is a question we cannot answer, for such an answer lies beyond the capabilities of present-day knowledge. And we cannot even define Platonism as the doctrine of Plato, for it is broader and deeper than this doctrine, even if it has found its best expression in Plato.

2. Ernst Laas, *Idealismus und Positivismus*, pt 1, Berlin, 1879, 5.

We have said "present-day knowledge." But is that really the case? Is it not true that the difficulty of answering the above question stems not only from the complexity of this phenomenon but also from its very nature? Since it is the point of departure of so many orientations of thought, each of which represents a high degree of breadth, can Platonism be anything else but a deep movement of the spirit whose name can only be a symbolic one that is clarified *per se*, not *per aliud* (through itself, not through another)? In this case, would it not be more correct to understand Platonism not as a definite and unchanging system of concepts and judgments, but as a certain kind of aspiration, as a divine finger pointing from earth to heaven, from things that are below to things that are above? In light of this we can understand that our soul's unquenchable aspiration toward the heavens, its flight toward other worlds, cannot be exhaustively defined by any fixed concepts or terms—for all things melt and flow when they touch the Truth, like wax when it comes into contact with fire.

Even in the case of Plato, each of the dialogues differs somewhat from every other dialogue with respect to orientation of thought and usage of the basic terms. This is even more evident in relation to other proponents of Platonism. But if the above question can only be answered in the affirmative, it becomes clear that the diversity of attempts to express Platonism's fundamental aspiration testifies not against but for this aspiration, that is, it attests to the richness and God-likeness of man. Then, the terms of Platonic systems of thought stop being terms in the strict sense but become living symbols of inner movements. We cannot impose an external order upon these symbols; however, a single integral life, a single suprarational center, beats in them like an all-harmonizing heart. Not knowing, or, more precisely, not knowing clearly and distinctly—that is, not being able to give a clear, verbal answer to the question of Platonism—we can however identify certain aspects of this extensive historical movement, of this primordial element of human life. In doing so, we will pay close attention to one of these aspects, to one of these symbols of Platonism.

But which one? Which symbol? I assume that when we pronounce the word "Platonism," we have in mind the association "idea, *eide*, doctrine of ideas, idealism."

2

Symbols
of Platonism

YOU WILL CLEARLY RECALL of course that the subject of our discussion concerns genera and species, as the philosophers of
antiquity used to say; *ousia*, *physis*, and *hypostasis*, terms formulated by patristic philosophers; *universalia*, an expression introduced by the western scholastics; or general concepts and
judgments, terms used by modern philosophers. All these
expressions refer to the same problem, formulated in different
geographical and temporal contexts. However, it is possible that
you do not grasp with equal clarity the deeply rooted content-
rich meaning of these disputes concerning *universalia*. My goal in
this lecture is to enable you to understand that what we are dis-
cussing refers, not to scholastic or pedantic verbosity, but to
extremely profound problems of metaphysics and epistemology,
and even of axiology. Thus, one's worldview, one's overall
understanding of life, depended on which solution of the problem of universals one accepted—Platonic or anti-Platonic. For
this reason, seemingly abstract and academic discussions of universals have served, serve, and will probably continue to serve
until the end of time as an arena of violent clashes and accusa-
tions of unorthodox thinking and heresy.

One historian remarks that "public disputes concerning universals would sometimes degenerate into virulent name-calling.
Courtesy and good manners were violated to such an extent that

popes and bishops had to issue strict decrees calling on the war-ring camps to cease hostilities."[1]

Another historian of thought points out that "it would be a great error to think that in the Middle Ages the question of the logico-metaphysical meaning of universals amounted to nothing more than a thought-exercise. The energy with which medieval science strove in endless debates to resolve this question (in com-plete independence from one another, the thought of the West and the thought of the East tackled this question with equal fer-vor) is itself sufficient proof that this question contains a real and very difficult problem."[2]

Therefore, the same historian, referring to such prominent allies as Lotze amd Libmann, declares that "to those contempo-rary scholars who consider the question of general concepts as nothing more than a curiosity that belongs in an archival dustbin, as nothing more than a childhood illness of science, to them—as long as they are not able to explain clearly and precisely the meaning of what they call the laws of nature—one must reply: *mutato nomine de te fabula narratur* (if the name is changed, the discussion turns out to be about yourself)."[3] Many other schol-ars are of the same opinion.

Another scholar points out that "the question of genera and species has in all epochs excited and fructified the human spirit and lay at the basis of all the schools. While taking on the hues of every particular epoch, it has remained the source and goal of philosophical inquiries. Outwardly, this question appears to con-cern only psychology and logic; but in its essence it dominates all philosophy, for there is no problem that fails to include the fol-

1. A. Stöckl, *History of Medieval Philosophy*, Russian trans, ed. I. V. Popov, Mos-cow, 1912, 262.

2. W. Windelband, *History of Philosophy*, Russian trans. P. Rudich, St. Peters-burg, 1898, pt 3, 265–66.

3. Ibid., 277, note 1.

lowing question: is it the case that all that we see is a combination of our mind, or does it have its basis in the nature of things?"[4] This means that all ontological or psychological doctrines must necessarily take into account the question of universals.[5] Maurice de Wulf remarks that "in rational philosophy the problem of universals is nothing other than the problem of the degree of truth of our intellectual knowledge."[6]

All this is perfectly true, but it is insufficient. The questions raised by idealism also have a much more general meaning.

---

4. Haureau, *De la philosophie scolastique*, Paris, 1850, 144–45.

5. As quoted in F. U. Uspensky, *Essays on the History of Byzantine Education*, St. Petersburg, 1892, 177–78.

6. Maurice de Wulf, "Le Problème des Universaux dans son évolution historique du IXe au XIIIe siècle," *Archiv für Geschichte der Philosophie*, Bd IX, Neue Folge, II Bd, 1896, 429.

3

Idealism and the
Theory of Knowledge

WHAT IS REAL? What is knowable? What is valuable? The present moment, experienced here and now; or something that, though it is correlated with the present moment, is eternal and universal? What is the foundation of life? What governs the activity of life? Is it governed by a metaphysical "*carpe diem*, seize the moment"? Or by a higher, otherworldly being? Is it the case that only that which is below truly exists? Or does that which is on high also exist, possessing a realer existence? And so on and so forth. Such are the questions which lie at the basis of the disputes over *universalia*. And every acknowledgement of the existence of the world on high leads to Platonism in one form or another, while adherence to the world below leads to the rejection of Platonism.

But before venturing into the thickets of these problems, let us consider only the problem of the theory of knowledge and logic. As you know, knowledge satisfies us if we are convinced of the universality and necessity of its results. Knowledge is knowledge only when it transcends the bounds of the given moment and given place, that is, when this singular moment is directed at otherworldly being, when it transcends its own bounds and signifies more than itself. If the whole thing is confined solely to this combination of psychic elements that does not transcend its own bounds, we regard it as a mere game of psychic processes and do not ascribe to it any cognitive significance. If I say that at the present moment I feel cold in this room, this statement does not have any scientific value, any cognitive significance. In order for such significance to arise, I must transcend the bounds of "myself," my "here" and "now," and expand at least in one direction beyond particular being. Knowledge exists only where *hen* expands to include *polla*, forming *hen kai polla* (the one and the many),[1] which is how Plato defines idea; knowledge exists only where "*mian . . . dia pollon* (one is among the many),"[2] which represents another one of Plato's definitions of idea; or, according to Aristotle's definition of idea, knowledge is possible where the one is directed toward the many, expands to include what is other—where "*to hen epi pollon* (the one is in the many)."[3] That is the formula used by medieval thought: *unum* is directed toward what is other, toward *alia*, which is how the scholastic philosophers phrased it; *unum versus alia* is, according to their etymology, *universale*—both singular and general.

But these ideas, these *universalia*, these general concepts and judgments, whatever we may call them (our contemporary logic recognizes them to be the same), possess enigmatic properties. The one refers to an infinite set, but "this infinite set of phenomena cannot be present as a set in the act of judgment, for a general judgment is a unique act of thought, not an accumulation of many judgments. Consequently, the question apparently becomes absolutely contradictory and takes on a paradoxical form: 'how can the infinite set of phenomena be present in a unitary act of thought?'"[4]

When I say "a horse is a vertebrate" or "in a right triangle the area of the square whose side is the hypotenuse is equal to the

1. *Sophist*, 253d.
2. *Philebus*, 14d, e, 15d.10.
3. Aristotle, *Metaphysics*, I (A) 9.
4. N. O. Lossky, *Grounding of Intuitivism*, 2nd ed. St. Petersburg, 1908, 240.

sum of the areas of the squares on the other two sides," I perform, here and now, an act of knowledge that in all respects is
unitary. I perform this act of knowledge now, here. But though it
is this bounded moment and place, it also overflows the limits of
its boundedness as it were and extends into the infinite distances
of time and space. Though it is unitary as an act, it, owing to its
content as an act of knowledge, possesses infinitude, for it states
that all horses, no matter where and when they have existed, are
such as it states them to be, i.e., vertebrates. In precisely the same
way, all right triangles, no matter where and when they are con-
ceptualized, are such that the Pythagorean theorem is valid for
them. The act of knowledge, of concept and judgment, is both
unitary and infinite; and it is this union of finiteness and infinitude, this contradiction of finiteness and infinitude, this inconfus-
ible and inseparable duality of the cognitive act, this antinomy of
the latter that constitutes the great enigma of universals. This
enigma can be divided into the three enigmas, the three problems
that correspond to the three disciplines in the light of which the
fundamental problem of duality can be examined. That is, the
fundamental question "How is such a duality possible?—is
divisible into three questions."[5]

First question: How is it possible psychologically? That is,
what psychological states must the subject of knowledge experience if they are to be both unitary and universal?

Second question: How is it possible metaphysically or, more
precisely, ontologically? That is, what real processes and things,
what objects of knowledge, must exist if there are to be general
judgments and concepts about them?

Third question: How is it possible gnoseologically? That is,
how can the general judgments of our reason have objective sig-

5. N. O. Lossky, *Introduction to Philosophy*, Part I, "Introduction to the theory of
Knowledge," St. Petersburg, 1911, 102–3.

nificance for things and processes? That is, how can they express properties of that which is not reason itself?

In order to understand how Platonism resolves these questions it is useful to draw a comparison with the resolutions offered by other intellectual currents. Though these problems have been the object of intense interest throughout the history of thought, from ancient to modern, and continue to be the object of intense interest, it is in the Middle Ages that they were debated with the greatest fervor; and so we will confine ourselves mainly to the medieval terminology.

4

Plotinus and
Neoplatonism

IF WE CONSIDER THE ESSENCE of the matter, we will find that the
debate about universals lay at the heart of ancient philosophy.
The antinomy of environment and individual—*hen kai pan* (the
one and the all)—stimulated Greek thought before Plato. After
the emergence of Plato's idealism, the debates about universals
became more clearly defined—both within the Academy, when
the founder of this idealism was still alive, and outside its walls.
In Plato's dialogues, especially some of the later ones, we
encounter statements directed against arguments in favor of the
theory of ideas, statements that are not always refuted. One is led
to think that such statements reflected a certain degree of agitated
confusion in Plato's school. Theoretical disagreements even
prompted Aristotle to leave the Academy and start his own
school. It was reported that, from that moment, hostile relations
arose between the two great philosophers, but these reports were
unproven and are deemed to be nothing more than gossip. However it is a fact that there were disagreements, disagreements precisely about the nature of ideas. These disagreements are not
great enough to prompt us to regard Aristotle as something other
than an idealist; however they are great enough to impel us to
regard the peripatetic theory of forms as a special type of idealism. Subsequently, the disagreements between various schools,
particularly regarding the question of ideas, become more acute.

The great unifier of the philosophy of antiquity, Plotinus, made a grandiose attempt to synthesize the various theories of ideas. Plotinus was not however only a great representative of the fading philosophy of antiquity but also a harbinger of the philosophy of the Middle Ages. The whole culture of antiquity was absorbed in Plotinus; meanwhile, the Middle Ages were not an accident but a legitimate progeny of ancient culture, which would allow us to regard Plotinus as a representative of medieval thought. This is reinforced by the fact that Plotinus had absorbed revelation to a greater extent than he realized; he had absorbed the Old Testament revelation through Philo and others (if not directly from the Septuagint), and the New Testament revelation from his teacher Ammonius Saccas and from the Gnostics with whom he polemicized. Furthermore, F. Picavet's careful analysis[1] concludes that Plotinus gives a "complete and systematic interpretation of the Apostle Paul's discourse in the Athenian Areopagus (Acts 17:16–34)." If that is the case, it would explain Plotinus' powerful influence on both patristic and scholastic thought. This would be the chief way in which the ancient theories of ideas were introduced into medieval thought; "ideas" turned out, in practice, to be much better suited to the Middle Ages than to antiquity.

But if one speaks not of the general influence of Neoplatonism on medieval philosophy, but of the particular impulse that put medieval thought in motion, one must first and foremost mention Plotinus' pupil Porphyry (233–304). Specifically, the point of departure for scholastic inquiries and debates about *universalia* can be found in that passage of Porphyry's "Introduction" to Aristotle's *Categories* which, by a happy historical accident, concisely formulates the crux of the debates in ancient philosophy

1. F. Picavet, *Plotin et Saint Paul* (Séances et travaux de l'Académie des sciences morales et politiques, Tome 61, 1904), 599–620.

regarding this subject. By some instinct, scholasticism focused its attention precisely on the central problem of ancient philosophy and, in a few lines, found the very gist of the debates, stretching over several centuries, between Plato and Aristotle, Plato and the Cynics, and the Academy, the Lyceum, and the Stoa. Here is the passage we have in mind "I set aside all discussion of genera and species, specifically all discussion of whether they exist independently or are found only in pure thought; and whether, if they exist independently, they are bodies or incorporeal; or whether they have existence in sensuous phenomena and with them; for such an discussion would take us into very profound depths and would require a very extensive investigation."[2]

2. Porphyry, *Isagoge et in Aristotelis Categorias commentarium*, 1 Band, 9–14.

5

Porphyry's Conception

FOR THE SAKE OF CLARITY, let us represent Porphyry's alternatives in the form of a diagram (see *Figure 1*).

τὰ γένη τε καὶ εἴδη

ὑφέστηκεν   ἐν μόναις ψιλαῖς ἐπινοίαις κεῖται

ἀσώματα   σώματα   χωριστά   ἐν τοῖς αἰσθητοῖς καὶ
περὶ ταῦτα ὑφεστῶτα

(*Figure 1*)

Universalia
exist

objectively or trans-   subjectively, solely in
subjectively as cognitive   reason, i.e., as *termini*
reason, i.e., *realia*

(*Figure 2*)

Realism   Terminism

before things   in things   as several concepts   as names or words
ante res   *in rebus*   *conceptus*   *nomina*
(*Platonism*)   (*Peripateticism*)   i.e., independently   i.e., not independently
of the sense and   of the sense and
content of words   content of words
(*Conceptualism*)   (*Nominalism*
Sermonism)

[19]

Translating this diagram into the language of medieval philosophy, and to some extent into the language of modern philosophy, we get a diagram (see *Figure 2*) that indicates the fundamental currents of thought, both medieval and later.

Comparing these two figures, we see that Porphyry's scheme contains different types of doctrines of *universalia* that have appeared in history with the exception of one where the existence of universals is denied. But since knowledge by its very essence is connected with the existence of universals, at least in some one sphere of being, it is clear that this doctrine must be cognitive nihilism, in the case of which the rejection of the universality of knowledge extends so far that even skepticism loses its meaning. In sum, one can represent this comparative analysis in *Figure 3*.

			Types of Doctrine							
			I	II	III	IV	V			
			Strict Realism	Moderate Realism	Concept-ualism	Nominalism Terminism	Nihilism			
Sphere of Being	1	IDEAS						Transsub-jective world		Layers of Being
	2	THINGS								
	3	CONCEPTS						Subjective world		
	4	TERMS								

(*Figure 3*)

However, *Figure 3* does not exclude—abstractly speaking—other solutions to the problem of universals. It is possible that the negation of universals proceeds not downward but upward (see *Figure 4*), so that doctrines emerge that recognize the existence of universals in the higher layers and deny their existence in the lower layers.

			Types of Doctrine						
			V′	VIII	VII	VI	I′	Transsubjective world	Layers of Being
Sphere of Being	1	IDEAS							
	2	THINGS							
	3	CONCEPTS						Subjective world	
	4	TERMS							

(*Figure 4*)

It would be hard to justify doctrines with this structure, but they are no stranger than doctrines of a nominalistic tendency. For example in the system of thought indicated as VI, one acknowledges the existence and knowability of Platonic ideas, but denies the adequate verbal expressibility of this knowledge. System of thought VII acknowledges the existence of ideas but denies their knowability and expressibility. Finally, system VIII acknowledges the existence of transcendent ideas but denies their appearance in the world and their knowability and expressibility. System of thought I′ represents Platonic realism. Formally, V′ is identical to nihilism, but, as the limit of striving toward the transcendent, i.e., being mystical agnosticism, it can be wholly other than sophistic nihilism V (e.g., as the acknowledgment of absolutely extra-creaturely, intra-divine thought).

Speaking abstractly, one can conceive of a number of other doctrines, i.e., combinations of negations and affirmations of universals in different layers of being. Since according to the combinatorial theorem, there must be 16 such combinations, and since we already have 8 of them, there remain 8 more abstractly possible types. Schematically, they are represented in *Figure 5*.

[21]

			Types of Doctrine									
			IX	X	XI	XII	XIII	XIV	XV	XVI		
Sphere of Being	1	IDEAS									Transsub-jective world	Layers of Being
	2	THINGS										
	3	CONCEPTS									Subjective world	
	4	TERMS										

(*Figure 5*)

Doctrine IX acknowledges the reality of universals in the world and outside it, but it indicates that they are unknowable, though they are expressed symbolically in words. Doctrine X acknowledges the reality of transcendent ideas as well as their knowability and expressibility, though it denies the existence of Aristotelian forms in the world. Doctrine XI acknowledges the existence of Platonic ideas and affirms that they are expressible in words, e.g., in poetry, but that things lack form and reason does not possess concepts. Doctrine XIII is purely metaphysical in nature. It allows universals as an object of pure thought, but these universals can reveal themselves neither in the world nor in word. And so on.

6

The One and the Many

THE PROBLEM OF *hen kai polla* is virtually the most fundamental *aporia* of philosophy, at least of Greek philosophy. The problems of individual and environment, continuity and discontinuity, *hypostasis* and *ousia*, and so on are all variants of this *aporia*. The negation of *polla* and *pan* in *hen* leads to the negation of knowledge, of the meaning of activity, and of the eternal in the temporal. The affirmation of *pan* and *polla* in *hen* requires one to explain how this is possible. The problem of universals is the apex of the fundamental problem of philosophy, and not to understand this is to understand nothing in philosophy.

Our aim is neither to refute various forms of "terminism" that seek to eliminate the aforementioned problem, nor to defend various forms of "realism" that seek to solve it in one way or another. That is not the task of the history of philosophy. Our aim is to attempt to clarify the meaning of various theories of universals. Let us sharpen our focus: What is the crux of the terminist tendency, and what is the crux of the realist tendency? For realism this crux is metaphysical and gnoseological egoism. Reality is absolutely solitary, absolutely outside everything that is not it. Reality is itself, nothing else. Reality lacks a navel, so to speak, which would bind it to the fruitful womb of total being. It lacks roots that would enable it to penetrate into other worlds. Finally, in time it is not connected with itself; in its existence it does not represent any integral or coherent being. The moment of the given state is connected with other moments neither onto-logically, nor in space and time; it does not penetrate into the depths, does not wear the crown of universality. The moment is only a moment, without the aroma, the atmosphere, of eternity. A point is only a point, without the anointment of universality. *Hen* is *hen* and only *hen* and in no possible way is it *polla* or *pan*. But if one immerses oneself in this perception of the world and asks what meaning does *hen* acquire here, the obvious answer must be that it refers to *I*. The true meaning of this orientation of thought is that I am I and only I, and in no possible way am I not I, Thou. I am not connected with anyone, not even with myself: *solus ipse sum,* and nothing concerns me or can concern me. Isolation, followed by egoism, followed by hatred, and ending in absolute nihilism—this is what lies at the basis of terminist theories. Terminism is heresy in the original and precise sense of the word.[1]

In contrast, realist theories come out of a sense of the kinship of all being, a sense of the non-absolute isolation of things, moments, and states, which is due not to their mechanical mixing or to the fuzziness of their definition, but to their inner kinship and unity. Not only is *hen* nonexclusively *hen*, but it is also *polla* and even *pan*. From *hen*, seen here and now, stretch innumerable threads to what is other, to *pan*, to universal being, to the fullness of being. These threads are living threads, creating out of an isolated and solitary *hen* the living organ of a living entity. *Hen* seems to be something self-enclosed and two-dimensional. But it only seems to be so. If you look at it closely, you will see that it is neither self-enclosed nor two-dimensional. It has a sweet fragrance. It is encircled by a halo whose rays are interwoven with

1. For the notion of heresy, see P. Florensky, *The Pillar and Ground of the Truth*, trans. Boris Jakim (Princeton: Princeton Univ. Press, 1997), 491–92.

the rays of other beings. It has depths with long roots penetrating into other worlds from which it receives life. Its tone is not the solitary, monotonous tone of a tuning fork, but a living harmony of many tones. Its content is infinitely richer than that of any rationalistic theory.

> Dear friend, don't you see
> That all we see is only
> A reflection and shadow
> Of what cannot be seen?
> Dear friend, don't you hear
>
> That this discordant roar Is
> Only a distorted echo
> Of joyous harmonies?[2]

True reality, idea, is not solitary being. It is *mian . . . dia pollon*, as Plato defines it, or *hen kai pollon*, as he declares, clearly hinting at the fundamental problem of Greek philosophy. Idea is, according to Aristotle, *to hen epi pollon*. The intuition of this *mian . . . dia pollon*, of this *hen kai pollon*, is the world-intuition that lies at the basis of idealism.

It is this antagonistic opposition of aspirations, on the one hand to isolate, to flatten, to make meaningless, and finally to annihilate the full-fledged seed of being, and on the other hand to let it sprout and bring forth a hundredfold increase, that is, to realize the inner beauty of creation; it is this opposition between the belief in death and the belief in life that constitutes the unceasing war between the terminist and realist tendencies, between positivism and idealism. The rest is philosophical tech-

---

2. A poem by Vladimir Solovyov.—Trans.

nique. The two tendencies are based on two different beliefs, or rather on belief and its negation. But both belief and non-belief strive to express themselves in detail and to erect defensive measures, seeking refuge in fortresses of complex systems of auxiliary concepts. Here, both in the domain of positivism and in the domain of realism, one can encounter different tactical moves, quarrels and disagreements, even internecine wars. However, the task of examining these controversies is of secondary importance.

Let us examine some positions of idealism. The first position, the most important one, arises when one discusses the problem of the roots of being and the connections of the world below with the world above in the proper and precise sense, i.e., the divine world. The problems of grace, sacraments and rituals, visions and prophecies, the Church, guardian angels, and so on, are points, listed almost arbitrarily, on this line of defense. You will note that the study of these points belongs, strictly speaking, to the domains of dogmatics and religious philosophy. Do not think that I have forgotten to put the word "Orthodox" in front of "dogmatics and religious philosophy." No, I have deliberately omitted this limiting attribute, for every dogmatics and every religious philosophy necessarily encounters the same problems and obtains one solution or another.

But, strictly speaking, closer to philosophy are the somewhat different formal problems that arise in discussions of the correlation of the individual *hen* with other individuals. The belief of realism that generates this correlation is expressed in its basic affirmation that individuals are not completely separate, that they are not as separate as it appears. But what does this affirmation mean? Generally speaking, the answer to this question is twofold, and this twofold answer generates a twofold understanding of the term *universale*, a twofold understanding of the word idea , i.e., of that in which individuals are not separate.

[26]

Let there be two individuals, A and B, e.g., two horses. What does it mean, from the point of view of the problem under discussion, that A and B, these two horses, are not separate? It means that horse A contains in some manner horse B and that horse B contains in some manner horse A. "In some manner" means that B is contained in A not in the same manner, absolutely not in the same manner that it is contained in itself. A particular interpretation of this "in some manner," i.e., a particular replacement of the indefinite in "some manner" by the definite "in a specific manner," gives a particular solution to the problem of universals.

What meaning can one attach to the non-separateness of horses A and B?

Horse A is characterized in our consciousness by the attributes: a', a'', a''', a supra (IV), ..., a supra (n). Horse B is characterized by the attributes: b', b'', b''', b supra (IV), ..., b supra (n).

Let us suppose that some of the attributes of the two series, i.e., the first three attributes, are identical. We have in mind not the similarity of the attributes but their identity by virtue of which horses A and B are similar. We must repeat that the matter at hand concerns not the similarity of the attributes, but their identity; if we were to speak of their similarity, we would necessarily encounter the question What makes them similar? And then this "what," this attribute of an attribute, would turn out to be identical in both attributes. But you might ask, What if here too, we would get only similarity? I would reply that then it would be necessary to speak of the attribute of an attribute that is identical. In general, either one must advance this series *ad indefinitum* and therefore fail to understand what makes the horses A and B similar, or one must interrupt the series at the term which would be recognized as identical in A and B. But the most natural thing would be to do this at once, finding this term directly in A and in B.

[27]

This notion has already been put forth. N. O. Lossky asks: "Can sameness of content exist in some relation without identity of content?" He answers: "... the notion of sameness and even of similarity in general inevitably leads to reference to the notion of identity or, if one does not desire to have recourse to this notion, it contains an infinitely repeating problem."[3] Here is what we find in Husserl: "Wherever we find sameness, we also find identity in the strict and true sense of the word. We cannot call two things the same without indicating in what aspect they are the same. It is this aspect in which identity is found. All sameness refers to the species to which the compared things are subordinate, and this species is not just something that once again is the same in both aspects, since in the contrary case we would inevitably get a *regressus in infinitum*. In describing the compared aspect, we indicate with the aid of a more general species term the circle of specific differences in which the identity of the compared aspects is found. If two things are the same in the aspect of form, the corresponding species of form is then the identical element in them; if they are the same in the aspect of color, the species of color is then the identical element in them, and so on. If anyone attempted to define—if only with respect to sense perceptions—identity as a limiting case of sameness, that would be a distortion of the true state of affairs. Identity, not sameness, is something absolutely indefinable. Sameness is a relation of objects subordinate to one and the same species. If one could not speak of the identity of a species, of that aspect in which sameness exists, one could not speak of sameness either."[4]

Thus, returning after the above digression to our discussion, we can affirm that, with respect to being, the attributes a', a'', a''' in A are numerically the same as b', b'', b''' in B. Just as we can

---

3. Lossky, *Grounding of Intuitivism*, 262.
4. E. Husserl, *Logische Untersuchungen*, part 2, Hall a. S., 1901, 112–13.

say that stars that are dissimilar but identical with respect to being shine over both Posad and Moscow and that students who are dissimilar but identical with respect to being appear in both Posad and Moscow, so we can say that the similarity attributes for A and B are identical. The combination of these attributes, or their logical product, forms a new essence—ω. It is ω that makes A and B inseparable. It is the thread that unites them. In logic ω is called the sum of A and B, for the sum here implies the alternative "either A or B." Let us clarify that we have in mind here the so-called "singular concepts," the individuals A and B, designated in logic as lA blB, and it is only for the sake of graphic simplicity that we write A and B. Using medieval terminology, we employ *haeccitates* ("thisnesses" or *Diesheiten*) of the objects A and B. But since, whether we have A or B, we have in both cases a$'$, a$''$, a$'''$, it follows that the alternative A or B defines ω: $\omega = A \sim B$.

But the question arises: Is this the only way one can conceive the non-separateness of A and B, or is there also another way? One clearly can take the logical product of A and B, and then one gets a new essence—Ω: $\Omega = A \sim B$.

This means "both A and B." Consequently, a$'$, a$''$, a$'''$ are taken here in an intensified manner; but, in addition, we get in Ω a supra (IV), ..., a supra (n), b supra (IV), ..., b supra (n). Consequently, ω turns out to be only a moment in the being of Ω. Then one can say that ω is the greatest common divisor of A and B, while Ω is the smallest common multiple, and in the sense of fullness of being we have the following gradation: $\omega < A < \Omega$; $\omega < B < \Omega$.

Realism asserts that ω (or, given other interpretations, Ω) is not only a method of thinking but also a reality, in the same way that the greatest common divisor (or the smallest common multiple) is a number, and not only a symbol of action like $<< + >>$ or $<< - >>$, $<< x >>$, $<< : >>$, i.e., a pure abstraction. But where and how does this reality ω (or Ω) exist? According to one interpretation, this is a foundation of things which does not exist if the things themselves do not exist, but without which the things cannot exist (Aristotle). According to another interpretation, it is a reality outside of things, existing for itself, but such that, in some manner, it is in things, or things are in it and cannot exist apart from it (Plato). At first glance, between Aristotle's forms and Plato's ideas lies an impassable chasm. But if one looks more attentively, one will see that the disagreement is not one of substance. This can be clarified by the example of metal shavings arranged in regular rows, demonstrating that they are interrelated through the deformation of a magnetic environment, the ether. Both Plato and Aristotle recognize this connection; but, further, there arises the question of what generates the magnetic field; and Aristotle answers that the shavings themselves are the source of the field, for, since they have an iron composition, they possess an intrinsic magnetism. Plato surmises, however, that the magnetic field is produced by a solenoid surrounding the shavings, and, since they have an iron composition, they are temporarily magnetized.

The Platonic conception is much broader than the Aristotelean one, which is a particular case of the Platonic one. Therefore, in some interpretations, the Platonic conception is very close to the Aristotelian one; in other interpretations, it is very distant from it.

As for choosing between ω and Ω, when they develop their own notions of idea or form, both Plato and Aristotle seem to speak of ω, but when they use ready-made notions, they speak of Ω as psychologically necessary, for if one conceives Ω as something like a Galton composite photograph, the combination of the general features of ω will appear in it with particular clarity. Ω differs from ω psychologically (not logically or ontologically) solely by the fact that ω appears sharply defined, whereas Ω

appears as the same ω, but accompanied by overtones, surrounded by an aura or atmosphere.

But, logically, ω and Ω are, of course, different. This is also the
case if we take not two individuals, but a certain finite plurality of
them: A, B, C, D, E, . . . , X, Y. Then we get:

$$\omega = A\sim B\sim C\sim D\sim E\sim \ldots \sim X\sim Y,$$
$$\Omega = A\sim B\sim C\sim D\sim E\sim \ldots \sim X\sim Y.$$

The more individuals we have, the more well-defined—psychologically—the central kernel of Ω will be, and the less well-
defined—psychologically—its surrounding aura will be, so that
the difference between Ω and ω becomes—psychologically—
less and less palpable. One can say, finally, that—psychologically—their limits are equalized:

$$\lim \omega = \lim \Omega$$
$$l = \infty \, l = \infty$$

It should be noted, however, that, logically and ontologically,
the difference between ω and Ω keeps growing.

But whether we understand *universale* as ω or as Ω (in essence
this is a terminological problem), we see that "realism is not an
explanation but a direct expression of facts directly experienced
in the act of stating a general judgment."[5]

In order to render the above outline of idealism less abstract,
we will present a number of considerations gleaned from our living experience. Platonic ideas would remain too formal a
gnoseological requirement if we did not attempt to show—not
them themselves—but at least something similar to them. To be
sure, every act of life is synthetic, as is, in particular, every act of
knowledge; and it is therefore permeated with the principle of
idealism. But in order to clarify idealism it is necessary to choose

5. Lossky, 247.

examples of the synthesizing principle of life in which the ideal would be manifested with particular clarity. In a brief lecture it is impossible to answer the question how ideas are possible psychologically, metaphysically, and gnoseologically, but it is possible, using concrete experiences, to show that, in the experience of life, the antinomy of ideas is by no means unexpected.

Our task, then, is not to defend idealism as a doctrine, but to clarify its meaning for the understanding of life in its conceptions and feelings. We now return to the point of our departure—life.

7

Idealism as an Embodiment of Life: Rodin

IDEALISM IS A "yes" to life, for life is an uninterrupted fulfillment of *hen kai polla*. What is the source of the theory of ideas? The best answer is that its source is living entity. Living entity is the clearest and fullest embodiment of idea. However, not every perception of a living entity (understanding this term in the sense of the Church Slavonic *zhivotno*, of the Greek *zoon*, or the Latin "animal") but only that which apprehends its life is a synthetic perception, transcending "here" and "now." Still photography artificially captures moment and place, creating an illusion of death and immobility. In contrast, an artist, having on swanlike wings flown beyond the double bound of space and time,[1] embodies movement in dead, immobile material, and thus the entity perceived by the artist shines through paints, marble, or bronze also for those who are capable of synthetic perception only to a lesser degree. An artist creates images of life. Thus, if one says that life is movement, one can legitimately say that works of art are images of movement. Whether we understand "movement" in the broad metaphysical sense, or in the narrow, mechanical sense, in both cases one can legitimately say that the antinomies of movement, so troubling for abstract rationality,

---

1. Not identified.—Trans.

are overcome by art. In order not to overwhelm the reader with examples, I will consider in detail the works and thoughts regarding the art of a single artist—Rodin.

"All of Rodin's works," Paul Gsell tells us, "palpitate with the truth of life; all of them are created out of flesh and blood; all of them breathe; but these two statues [the 'Age of Bronze' and 'John the Baptist'] move."[2] "It is as if some mysterious force gives life to the bronze."[3] He asks: "What brings these immobile bronze or stone masses to life, giving them the power of movement and even making them capable of strenuous effort?"[4] Rodin himself supplies the answer: "Movement is nothing but the transition from one position to another."[5] The artist "represents the transition from one position to another; he indicates how one pose is imperceptibly transformed into another. In his work you discern what has happened in the past and guess what will happen in the future."[6] An example of this is Rodin's statue of Marshal Ney. "The hero pulls out his saber and with a thunderous shout orders his regiment to advance." If we look at the statue attentively, we remark the following: "The Marshal's legs and the hand holding the scabbard remain in the same position they were in when he was pulling out the saber; his left leg is moved to the side, making it more convenient for his right hand to pull out the saber; his left arm remains in the air, as if still raising the scabbard."

"Look at the torso," Rodin invites us. "In order to accomplish the movement we have described, the torso must shift again to the left; then it straightens up; the chest is thrust forward; the

2. A. Rodin, *Art. A series of conversations recorded by P. Gsell*, Russian trans. St. Petersburg, 1913, 48.
3. Ibid., 50.
4. Ibid., 50–51.
5. Ibid., 53.
6. Ibid., 53–55.

head turns toward the soldiers; with thunderous voice the hero gives the command to attack, and finally, the right arm is raised and swings the saber." Thus, the movement of the statue consists in the transformation of the Marshal's first pose, where he pulls the saber out of the scabbard, to the following pose, where with raised saber he rushes at the foe. That explains the whole mystery of the gestures conveyed by art: the sculptor compels the viewer to follow the development of gestures on the figure represented.

"In the above example, our eyes naturally look upward, from the legs to the raised arm, and since as they do so, they encounter other parts of the statue represented in consecutive moments, an illusion of ongoing movement is produced."[7]

Likewise, in the "Age of Bronze," "the movement appears to be upward. The youth has just awakened but his legs are still in a state of slumber and seem to tremble; as the viewer's gaze is raised upward, the whole figure is solidified: the ribs are visible beneath the skin, the chest cavity expands, the face turns toward the sky, and the arms stretch out to shake off the slumber. The subject of this statue is transition from slumber to the force of life which is on the verge of being transformed into movement."[8]

In "John the Baptist," "the rhythm is one of a change of equilibrium. The figure, which at first seems to rest solidly on its left foot, appears to start rocking when our gaze turns rightward. It seems that the whole body is leaning in this direction; then the right foot moves forward and stomps on the ground. At the same time the left shoulder is raised as if in an effort to shift the weight of the body to its side and enable the back leg to move forward. The sculptor's art consists in the ability to compel the viewer to feel all these moments in consecutive order and, by combining

7. Ibid., 55–56.
8. Ibid., 57.

them, to obtain the impression of movement."[9] In contrast, a still photograph of walking people does not give the impression of movement. "They stand motionlessly on one leg or they hop along. Both feet of John the Baptist rest on the ground, but what happens if you tell a model to imitate the movement of the sculpture and you then take a still photograph? The back leg is raised in the air, while the foot of the other leg has not yet touched the ground. You get the bizarre figure of a man afflicted by paralysis and frozen in this position. A figure captured by still photography appears to be frozen in the air because all the parts of its body are captured in a split second; unlike in art, there is no progressive development here."[10]

We will not further inquire into how an artist represents more complex movements, entire processes, and developing events. But we will ask which is capable of capturing more reality: a camera lens or an artist's eye, a photosensitive plate or an artist? "An artist is right, whereas a photograph lies," Rodin replies, "because time does not stop, and if an artist succeeds in conveying the impression of a gesture lasting several instants, his work will certainly be much more real than a scientific image in which the flow of time is suddenly interrupted."[11] What is represented on a photograph is infinitely poorer in reality than what is represented on a painting or in a sculpture, for the photographic representation is a fiction. If we say that the artistic representation is the reality, we would have to accept Viacheslav Ivanov's formula according to which artists and poets ascend from "*a realibus ad realiora*" (from what is real to what is most real),[12] for compared to the world of sense perceptions, works of art are *entia realiora*.

9. Ibid., 58–59.
10. Ibid., 61–87.
11. Ibid., 61–62.
12. V. Ivanov, *Guided By the Stars*, St. Petersburg, 1909, 277.

In other words, the world of ideas or universals shines through works of art.

Thus, in representing the body, art captures life in the aspect of its relatively external movement. In contrast, representations of the face reflect movements which are more inner and subtle. As a further step in clarifying the nature of ideas, we will quote what Christiansen has to say on the esthetic problem of the portrait.

8

The Esthetic Problem
of the Portrait

"First question: how does a portraitist give life to his subject?
Of the depicted head the first thing we require is that it live. The
face must be intensely alive; and the more intense its life, the better the portrait is. We have a low opinion of photographic portraits not only because their esthetic value is low but also because
they are insufficiently alive, and when they do capture life, it is
by accident. Photographic portraits capture an isolated moment
of time, giving it duration and producing an impression of something petrified and lifeless: the continued existence of a single
petrified moment is a negation of life. . . ."[1]

What is life? Its opposite is petrifaction, the immobile duration
of the identical. Therefore, for life to exist, it is necessary to have
a sequential change of non-identical states. A portraitist must
capture this sequentiality in a picture, a sequentiality which,
however, must continue to exist in the form in which it was created.

This raises the question: how can a process occurring in time,
how can change and movement—i.e., life—be represented in a
picture in such a way that the viewer sees it as a succession of
non-identical states?

---

1. B. Christiansen, *Philosophy of Art*, Russian trans. G. Fedorov, St. Petersburg,
1911, Part VIII, 281–89.

A portrait requires life which is dominated by repose, life which has duration and compels you to stop in front of it, life which holds you in quiet contemplation. The hurried daubings and distortions of the Impressionists allow only a hasty glance and fail to capture what is most substantial in painting. In particular, the Impressionist approach contradicts the tranquil flow of the life of the soul that a portrait requires.

And so, the Impressionist approach is not suitable here. Other approaches are needed, as is demonstrated by the works of the great master-portraitists of Holland, Germany, and Italy. When we stand before such a portrait and try to understand how its life is communicated, it appears to us that the expression of the face keeps changing; we notice that one mood is succeeded by another, which is succeeded, perhaps, by the first one and then by a new one, and so on—a tranquil succession in which, however, we hear again and again one fundamental tone.

Comparing portraits, we will perhaps also find that the life in them has a particular relation to their size: as the size of a portrait increases, we get not only an increase in the fullness of its life but also an increase in the decisiveness with which various features are represented, starting with the evenness of the subject's gait. Portraitists know from experience that a larger head "speaks" more lightly. As we continue our scrutiny, we notice that our gaze wanders back and forth over the portrait: from eyes to mouth, from one eye to the other, and to all the moments constituting the expression of the face; our gaze palpates the shapes of the features, weighs the relation of the surfaces, and continually returns to the eyes, resting there after all its wanderings. We think there may be a connection between this wandering of our gaze and the necessary size of the portrait: a larger field of view enables the gaze to detach itself completely from a single point and to move freely in all directions; such a wandering is even necessary if we are to gather all the elements of the whole. The intensity of life in a portrait will therefore depend on the calmness and amplitude of the contemplating and gathering movement of the gaze.

Furthermore, we find that, from the different points of view at which it sequentially stops, our gaze assimilates different moments, different facial expressions and moods, but all of them fall into agreement, like complementary colors or harmonically measured sounds. As the gaze wanders, it seems as if the portrait's expression and mood change; a harmonious sequentiality is produced.

We are now able to pinpoint the technique used by great painters to give life to a portrait: *the physiognomic disharmony of the different factors of facial expression.* It would seem that, abstractly speaking, it would be much more natural for artists to represent the same mood in the corners of the mouth, in the eyes, and in other details of the face, uniformly expressing the life of the soul in the melody of the contours, the colors, and all the other forms. The whole portrait would then be like a single, unique tone intensified by all the resonances, but life would be absent in it. The artist therefore differentiates the manner in which the soul is expressed in the face, making the expression of one eye somewhat different from that of the other, the expression of one corner of the mouth different from that of the other, and so on over the whole face. But simple distinctions are insufficient; among them it is necessary to have a harmonious relationship. Among them there must exist what, in the analysis of style, has been called the "separation of functions."

Among them there must exist a teleological tension which would make it possible to move from the definition of the goal to the goal itself, for this process is an essential condition of a work of art. They must therefore be differentiated in such a manner that one of the factors of expression dominates the process and becomes the end of the movement. The eyes are key here; they must be given an expression which serves as the fundamental tone and complement of every other physiognomic or formal factor.

The main melodic theme of the face depends on the relation between eyes and mouth.

The folds of the mouth reflect the intensity of will power, while the eyes reflect the resolving tranquility of the intellect. Portraitists throw the arc of least tension from one eye to the other. They give the eyes different emotional expressions; one of the eyes is accentuated and marked as the end-point, making the teleological relation definite and irreversible.

Other factors of facial expression, too, can become a counter-weight to the emotional content of the dominant eye, as can everything else that expresses the particular language of individual forms. Our eye then slides, again and again departing from its point of rest, and finds new stimuli and questions which, through its return, are resolved in its fundamental tone. And in its wide, tranquil movement back and forth, the eye gathers the rhythm of the sequence of intensities and resolutions, promises and fulfillments, which we experience as the tranquil breathing of healthy life.

So, our inquiry into the problem of the portrait, i.e., essentially the problem of the face, brings us closer to an understanding of idea as a kind of *hen kai polla*, as a kind of infinite synthesis or "infinite unit" (to use Father Serapion Mashkin's term). Indeed, what is the face of a person if not the element through which his idea becomes visible? To represent a person's face in a portrait is to make this person's idea accessible to external apprehension.

There are many examples which show that "thinking about the general is not always thinking about class."[2] In other words, a work of art provides, if not proof, at least a reason to think that a unit can be not only an individual singularity (*individuelle Einzel-*

2. Lossky, 286.

heit), but also a general singularity (*specifische Einzelheit*), to use the terminology of a present-day realist, Husserl.[3] The eternal and universal is present before the viewer of images of art, though they are more concrete and individual than the concreteness and individuality of sensory representations.

> This leaf, dried up and fallen,
> Is aflame in song like eternal gold,[4]

says the poet; and his words apply to all art, for art raises reality to the heavenly heights, to its eternal prototypes, leading us *a realibus ad realiora*.

3. Husserl, 146–48.
4. Not identified.

9

Hinton and the
Higher Consciousness

THE SYNTHETIC CHARACTER and, therefore, the reality of an image of art are effected through the merging of impressions from the object, i.e., through the unification into a single apperception of that which is given in different moments and therefore from different angles of view. It should not be thought, however, that this overcoming of time is exclusively a property of esthetic perception, though this property receives particular emphasis in esthetic perception. No perception is possible without the participation of memory, and the essential significance of memory has repeatedly been demonstrated by different methods and in different orientations, from Kant to our own day. If that is the case, every perception, as an act of life, overcomes time and therefore is synthetic; this is true for every perception, not only for *hen*, but also for *polla*, and, in some sense, even for *pan*. The latter, i.e., the universality of every perception, is certain, for the totality of our psychic life is the condition of every given perception, and none of them is given in isolation, in separation from the background of experience—which again has been demonstrated repeatedly, from Kant to the psychologists of our own day.[1]

If that is the case, if every perception is a synthesis of what is perceived in different moments and from different angles of

1. See P. Florensky, *The Pillar and Ground of the Truth*, 509–10.

[45]

view, the following question arises: Is it not possible that this synthetic character can be extended significantly further? Is it not possible—through the appropriate exercise and consequent development of the apperceptive capacity—to produce a clear synthesis of what is perceived at moments very remote from one another and from very different angles of view?

Let us assume that we observe a certain cube and sequentially move around its six sides. Or that we sequentially turn all six of its sides. Is it possible to transform this series of sequential impressions of the cube, obtained from different angles of view, into a single integral perception? In other words, is it possible to have a single synthetic perception of the cube from all of its sides? Or, going further, is it possible to obtain a synthetic perception of the cube as a single whole, both externally and internally?

Our answer to these questions is "Why not?" Especially since, in dreams and visions, we often encounter cases where the same object is viewed both from outside and from inside at the same time, or from different sides. Moreover, a number of direct experiments appear to have revealed the first glimmers of a new perception; specifically, we have in mind the experiments of the American investigator C.H. Hinton[2] on the development of what he calls a "higher consciousness." His method is not complicated. It involves "a long series of exercises ... with differently colored cubes which must be remembered in one position, then in another, and then in a third, and then imagined in new combinations."[3] Thus, the first experiment consists in the examination of a cube made up of 27 smaller cubes, differently colored and with different names.

2. See C.H. Hinton, *A New Era of Thought*, London, 1900.
3. N.D. Uspensky, *The Fourth Dimension*, St. Petersburg, 1910, 8.

In carefully examining this composite cube, we must turn it over and examine it (i.e., try to remember it) in reverse order. Then we must turn over the little cubes in a certain manner and remember them in this order. As a result, in the composite cube we can nullify the notions of up and down, left and right, etc., and know it independently of the mutual position of the little cubes, i.e., visualize them simultaneously in different combinations... Then a description is given of a long system of exercises with series of differently colored and named cubes, composing different figures.[4]

Thus, according to Hinton, as a result of the exercises it should be possible to produce an "impersonal" representation of the spatial world, i.e., a representation not connected with any single point of view and therefore without perspective. This possibility of a new synthesis can be called a representation in four-dimensional space. In fact, the properties of such a representation coincide with the properties of four-dimensional space formally derived in multidimensional geometry. Perspectiveness, i.e., in essence, the distortion of the world of representations, depends on the three-dimensionality of space as a form of perception. Therefore, it is natural to attempt to transition to four-dimensional perception through the learned habit of mentally correcting every three-dimensional perception. In essence, this is the same manner in which the possibility of a new synthesis transitions from perspective-distorted two-dimensional perception to three-dimensional perception, for the perspectiveness of the world of representations is a kind of mental addition to two-dimensional perception.

In the same way that we learn three-dimensional perception, a special training enables us to achieve four-dimensional perception. "Hinton's idea consists in the fact that, before thinking of

4. Ibid., 8, note.

developing the capacity of vision in the fourth dimension, it is necessary to imagine how objects would look from the fourth dimension, i.e., not in perspective but at once from all sides, the way our consciousness knows them. The goal of Hinton's exercises is to develop this capacity. According to Hinton, the nullification of the personal element in the representations must lead to a nullification of the personal element in the perceptions. Thus, the development of the capacity of imagining an object from all sides is the first step in developing the capacity to see objects as they are, i.e., in developing what Hinton calls higher consciousness."[5]

5. Ibid., 9, note.

10

Picasso

In HINTON'S EXPERIMENTS, as in similar methods, it is impossible not to feel that something artificial is imposed on the spiritual organism. There is no doubt that such methods produce real results and are therefore highly edifying for the philosopher; but one can scarcely deny that these methods are unnatural, so that the function extracted by them from outside is not produced through life-activity, is deprived of inner force, and is therefore unconnected with integral life. Thus, the abuse of such experiments, the artificial creation of possibilities which should arise naturally, leads to the sickness and degeneration of the person.[1]

---

1. Bishop Ignatii Brianchianinov presents a very profound discussion of the mystical unfeeling of sinners: "People become capable of seeing spirits when they experience a certain alteration in their senses, an alteration which occurs in an unnoticeable and inexplicable manner for the person. He only notices that he has suddenly started seeing what he has not seen before and what other people do not see; or he starts hearing what he has not heard before. For those who experience such an alteration, it is quite simple and natural, though it is inexplicable for oneself and for others; for those who have never experienced it, it is strange and incomprehensible. Everyone knows that people are capable of drifting off into sleep, but it remains a mystery how we pass from a state of alertness and wakefulness to a state of slumber and self-forgetfulness. The alteration of the senses in the case in which a person enters into sensory contact with entities of the invisible world is what the Bible calls the opening of the senses." This is followed by allusions to the opening of the senses in the story of Balaam, in the experience of Elijah, and in the journey to Emmaus. "From the cited passages of the Bible," the Bishop continues, "it is clear that the corporeal senses serve as the doors and gates leading into the inner cell where the soul abides and these gates are opened and closed depending on God's

We can find a vivid example of this kind of artificial transition to other forms of perception in the works of Pablo Picasso. Among the different stages of the artistic path of this still-young experimenter on himself and on the world, we are most interested in the most recent stage where the poisoned soul of this important artist creates images of four-dimensional perception, in which, however, there is no sense of authentic life. I have in mind his series of musical instruments, splendidly exhibited in the Moscow Shchukin paintings gallery.

---

will. These gates remain wisely and mercifully closed in fallen human beings so that our sworn enemies, the fallen spirits, do not penetrate into us and harm us. This measure is made the more necessary because, after having fallen, we abide in the realm of fallen spirits, surrounded by them and enslaved by them. Not having the opportunity to penetrate into us, they communicate with us from outside, stirring up various sinful thoughts and reveries designed to infect our weak souls. It is not permissible for a person to dispense with God's watchfulness and, against God's will, to open one's senses and come into direct contact with spirits. But it happens. It is clear that, with one's own resources, one can achieve contact only with fallen spirits. It is improper for holy angels to participate in a matter contrary to God's will, in a matter not pleasing to God. What attracts human beings to open contact with spirits? Those who are thoughtless and ignorant of active Christianity are attracted by curiosity, lack of knowledge, and lack of faith, not knowing that by coming into such contact they can cause great harm to themselves." (*The Works of Bishop Ignatii*, vol. 3, 13–15)

"No benefit comes from seeing the Lord with corporeal eyes," the Bishop says in another place, "when the mind is blind and faith, this power of spiritual vision, is inactive. But when faith is active, the Heavens are opened and the Son is seen at the right hand of the Father. Unfeeling and blind are corporeal eyes when the mind is blind. When He abided on earth, our Lord Jesus Christ accomplished amazing miracles in confirmation of His Divinity. These miraculous signs were so certain and convincing that the Divinity of the incarnate God had to become obvious for the most limited and sensuous people. But people gazed with wide-open eyes and saw nothing. The Evangelist John, as though amazed and bewildered, as though lamenting and pitying his contemporaries, declares: 'But though he had done so many miracles before them, yet they believed not on him'. (John 12:37) Further, the Evangelist identifies the cause of this blindness: the darkening of minds and the hardening of hearts produced by a life of sin and making it impossible for human eyes to see the Truth." (Ibid., vol. 4, 277–78)

This is how one artist characterizes this stage of Picasso's development: "Starting in 1910 he begins to incorporate principles of divisionism, dynamism, and complementarism into his painting. At this point, division of the object into parts becomes a necessary element in his paintings. By separating the object into several pieces, he recreates it in a new and unusual form. In turning toward the viewer different sides of these parts, front or back, inner or outer, Picasso arranges them on the canvas not arbitrarily but on the basis of the new principles adumbrated above; the spirit of construction dominates here too, but now we see the objects of his paintings represented simultaneously from several points of view, and we grasp them more fully and deeply and in a completely new way. In his *Nature morte* he divides a violin into its component parts, as if looking inside it, and he arranges these parts on the canvas not at random but following a predetermined principle according to which the interaction of the objects' plastic masses is delineated more deeply. Out of the violin's component parts he constructs a whole which reveals in a more all-sided and plastic manner the violin's inner life, its rhythm and dynamic force.

"Hitherto, Picasso had conveyed movement as a static phenomenon, as one of a continuous series of instantaneously fixed movements; but now his goal is to depict in a painting the sensation of movement itself. Picasso is a profound painter; the new method acquires particular power and persuasiveness in his works; the works done in this style ('Le Compotier' and 'The Violin') convey the impression of something profound and finished."[2]

2. A. Grishcheno, *Relationship of Russian Painting with Byzantium and the West in the 13th to 20th centuries*, Moscow, 1913, 80–81.

11

Four-Dimensional Perception

THE NOTION OF THE POSSIBILITY of four-dimensional perception has been formulated repeatedly; and it is quite possible that this notion is an integral element of the understanding of life and therefore is as ancient as that whole with which it is essentially associated. At any rate, the religious symbolism of the most ancient religions comes to life when we view it in the light of the four-dimensional notion. Ancient philosophers expressed with great clarity the notion of four-dimensional reality. Let us recall Plato's "myth of the cave." Even as shadows, the two-dimensional schemata and projections of things refer to bodies, so the three-dimensional world refers to the true world. That is how Plato explains the mystery of the cave perceptions. This mystery has its source in the Diktaean cave on Crete, which served as a refuge for the newly born Zeus.

Subsequently, cave mysteries have repeatedly been an object of philosophical inquiry, up to and including Schelling and Goethe. But Ideas, the Mothers of all existing things, live in the depths, i.e., in the depth direction of our three-dimensional world, and therefore all speech regarding them, even the most coherent, remains—for three-dimensional ears—nothing more than "the jabbering gibberish of the Parcae."[1]

---

1. From Pushkin's poem "Insomnia."—Trans.

However, regarding the depths of the world, which are discovered when the soul is ordered rightly, it is not only possible but necessary to speak. "I bow my knees unto the Father of our Lord Jesus Christ, of whom the whole family in heaven and earth is named, that He would grant you, according to the riches of his glory, to be strengthened with might by his Spirit in the inner man; that Christ may dwell in your hearts by faith; that ye, being rooted and grounded in love, may be able to comprehend with all saints what is the breadth, and length, and depth." (Eph. 3:14–18)

Not less ancient is the association of the question of the depth of the world with the problem of time. As early as Plato, in his definition of time as "the moving image of eternity," we can discern a hint at another mystery of the cave. Transposed into the world of science, this mystery was later called the "kinetic theory of time"[2] and now, in the modern electromagnetic world-picture, it is called the principle of relativity. But vain are these attempts of the world to catch the soul in its killing nets; only the outer shell of the soul is caught in them, while the mystery of life, like a moving wave, hides in the darkness of the cave. Neither Picasso, that desecrator of life, nor the self-satisfied scientists with their mechanisms and tools, even when they move at a micrometric pace, are capable of extracting this treasure; for when the lovers of death come in search of it, it hides even more deeply in the dear recesses of the Earth. In the end, this treasure can be found only if it is one's own.

We now return to the theme of our inquiry. Once again, what does it mean to "see an idea"? According to Plato, it means to see that "*hen ta polla einai kai to hen polla*,"[3] i.e., that "the many is the one and the one is the many"; or to see the union of "*tou aperiou*

<hr />

2. See M. Aksyonov, *Transcendentally Kinetic Theory of Time*, Kharkov, 1896.
3. *Philebus*, 14e.

kai peratos,"[4] i.e., of the limitlessness of the entity and the bound-edness of the concretely given. How does this seeing become possible in the case of four-dimensional perception?

Psychology asserts that we actually see the world as two-dimensional and that it gets its relief from constant corrections of the sensory material by unconscious ratiocination. The three-dimensional depth of the world is qualitatively other than what we have in the two-dimensional case. If we imagine what a two-dimensional perception would look like, we would see only lin-ear segments, and the curvature of the lines, i.e., the depth of the world in two dimensions, would be produced by an intellectual correction associated, in this case too, with unconscious ratioci-nation.

You will tell me that this is a fiction. But I will reply that it is not so remote from everyday reality as it may appear at first glance. We are all slightly afflicted with this "fiction," inasmuch as for us, for everyone, the first dimension and the second are not given with equal weight. I am thinking of visual astigmatism. If you consider an eye with extreme astigmatism, you will find that the image produced by it will consist of a series of parallel lines. Every line that is perpendicular to the direction of the lens axis will be invisible, and therefore we would be unable to imagine the possibility of lines perpendicular to the bundle of parallel lines that will be the sole object of our experiment.

If that is the case, we would not be able to imagine the mea-sure of distance between the parallel lines and therefore we would not be able to imagine the distance either, for the latter is given by the perpendicular line; i.e., intellectually, all the parallel lines will merge into one. Thus, we will *see* only a straight line; the intellectual correction will give it depth in two dimensions

4. Ibid.

and will make us inhabitants of a two-dimensional world. What will we see in this two-dimensional world?

For the sake of clarity, let us imagine a plane intersecting the three-dimensional world and giving a section of the world in the form of systems of images, lines, and points. Let us imagine that the object of this kind of sectioning is a tree. Its branches will give elliptical and circular sections; its leaves will give quasi-linear segments; its fruits and blossoms will give more complex planar structures. The result will be many mutually independent planar "objects." They will be the *polla*. In studying the morphology of these objects, an observer will classify them as green linear segments with tiny convexities, white ellipses (imagine that we are talking about birches), and green ellipses. He will construct several "general concepts," and this will be an important scientific achievement.

Observing the life-processes and the cotemporality of different structures and perhaps studying the chemical properties of the sap, some brilliant botanist will recognize the unity according to type of organization of the leaf projections and branch projections, and will perhaps develop an evolutionary theory which will recognize the unity of the origin of all the forms and suggest a genealogy of the leaves arising from a proto-branch. Connectedness in time is the highest flight of thought our astigmatic botanist would be capable of. And would it not be considered a fantastic and unscientific delirium if some "mystic" would suggest that all these organisms are not successively one, but *really* one, and that there is a higher unity, a *Hen* in which they are not just thought, but *seen* as organs? Perhaps, artists in this two-dimensional world would attempt to creatively synthesize an image composed of the leaves and branches?

But their obscure dreams would probably remain absolutely incomprehensible to the "planar" society and to the "planar" art critics, even though these dreams might awaken in these critics a dissatisfaction with their two-dimensional perception. But let us now imagine that the eye lens of one of the observers would start to curve in the direction of the axis. Then the observer would start becoming conscious of a new dimension of space, first obscurely and then in the measure of the equalization of the curvature radii of the principal sections of the lens, and the seeing would become clearer and clearer.

When the lens takes the form normal for human beings, one of the observers would suddenly see the tree as a whole. In that which he would see, there would be nothing resembling what he had seen earlier; this would be a qualitatively new perception. But this qualitatively new perception would contain the earlier perception, which would be one of the innumerable moments of the fullness of the latter. The relation between the new and the old perceptions would therefore be irreversible, while there would be a natural transition from the higher to the lower; the transition from the lower to the higher could only occur miraculously.

Back to us. It may be that our lens is linear with respect to the fourth dimension and we lack the ability to see and be conscious of the four-dimensionality of the world. In that case, the multiplicity of similar objects can be explained by their projectedness, i.e., by the three-dimensional projection of a four-dimensional object that is one. But as soon as our eyes are opened and the world is seen to possess *depth*, we will see the forest as one being, all horses as one super-horse, and humanity as Comte's *Grand Étre*, the Kabbalah's *Adam Kadmon*, or Nietzsche's *Übermensch*.[5]

5. Nietzsche's notion of the superman has two opposite tendencies. One of these, arising later and probably resulting from his illness, is individualistic, whereas the earlier one, expressed primarily in Zarathustra, is universalistic and closely resembles the mystical doctrine of the Heavenly Man; cf. Swedenborg's doctrine of the Body of Christ, expounded in his treatise, "On the heavens, on the world of spirits, and on hell."

But Forest, Horse, and Humanity resemble forest, horse, and human being to a far lesser degree than forest, horse, and human being resemble their micrometric sections.

One who knows the higher essence has a greater understanding of the lower essence than one who knows only the lower essence; the higher essence is absolutely unknowable for one who knows only the lower essence. This can be compared to the identification of a person from his fingerprints.

There is a real connection between the individuality of a person and the form of his dermal papillae, the analysis of which is now employed in criminal investigations. But could a two-dimensional being, even a very intelligent one, understand that prints left on his plane come from one particular individual and indicate a unity? It would be even less possible for this being to imagine the form of this unimaginable three-dimensional individual. When his thought reaches the highest point of its flight, he might be able to postulate the existence of this three-dimensional individual, but only as a hypothesis of his thought which has no concrete correlative in his experience.

A multidimensional form in the world—or, more precisely, in experience—of a lesser number of dimensions cannot be perceived as a whole; because of its higher degree of reality, because of the "*realiora*" of the fullness of its content, it cannot be confined within the too narrow frame of our being. But this impossibility does not exclude its sequential perception as a series of individual moments of its being, or as a series of micrometric sections which, while not giving a concrete representation of the one whole of which they are forms. nevertheless give an abstract notion of it. The sequence of the passage of this series of moments is what links the multidimensional space with time, which therefore turns out to be a kind of equivalent of the fourth dimension, or, if you will, the fourth coordinate.

Thus, every process can be regarded not as an internal change of that which changes, but as the passage of a multidimensional object through a three-dimensional space, and the phases of development can be regarded not as successive stages, but as cotemporal bounds in the being of this object. If, for example, on the plane of a point-embryo, a little circle develops which begins to grow and then, having reached a certain maximum value, shrinks and, being compressed back into a point again, vanishes from our experience—if this happens, then, in the planar world, this process can be understood as the passage of a size-invariant three-dimensional sphere through the plane of experience.

Similarly, a little star that appears suddenly, grows unusually quickly in magnitude and size, and then vanishes no one knows where—this star can be a four-dimensional star, a fiery hypersphere, or a so-called "sphero-sphere"[6] flying through our three-dimensional world. And new stars that explode suddenly and soon vanish, sometimes forever—these stars, usually viewed as cosmic catastrophes, may in fact be hyper-stars appearing in the sky of three-dimensional space. The notion examined here is in essence familiar to everyone inasmuch as it lies at the basis of the genetic method for investigating reality. To understand a phenomenon as a whole, instead of separating out from it one moment and focusing all one's attention on it, one can capture all the stages of its development in their totality. To understand something by collecting and integrating the moments of its appearance—that is precisely what we mean when we regard time as the fourth coordinate of a phenomenon and the phenomenon itself as four-dimensional. We say that an individual, one and identical to himself, is known in his biography; but can this self-contradictory assertion mean anything else except the fact that the individual cannot be exhausted by any particular moment

6. A term coined by N. Gulak-Artemovsky. See *Geometry in Four Dimensions*, 1877.

in being, i.e., by his supra-empirical nature? Every moment of the biography of a given individual is the sectioning of his reality by empirical space, i.e., by a lower-order reality.

The individual himself, in his wholeness, is not perceived concretely but is thought abstractly as the synthesis of all the moments of his biography. This unity exists not in time (at least, not in our order of time) but in that which (relative to our time) can be called eternity, though not in the absolute sense.

From this it is clear that every religion, always seeking a higher reality, postulates eternity—of one order or another. Both aspirations are expressed in the creation of symbolic syntheses, without which virtually no religion is possible. We will examine only a couple of examples of such symbol creation.

We can find a vivid example of such synthetic forms tied to religious symbolism in the "tree of life" or "sacred tree" (*der heilige Baum, der Lebensbaum*; *l'arbre sacre, l'arbre de vie*) of Babylonian and especially Assyrian art. What exactly is it?

For Le Comte Goblet d'Alviella this tree represents the most ancient image of the "Tree of Worlds" (*l'Arbre de mondes*) or the "Cosmogonic Tree" (*l'Arbre cosmogonique*). The meaning of this image is easy to interpret. It is an image of life in its totality, i.e., the idea of life.

This tree has been compared with the Tree of Life in the Book of Genesis. The Assyrian-Babylonian tree is thought to express the idea of the fullness of life, the center into which all life is gathered; meanwhile, the tree in Genesis represents the superabundant source of life whose fruits, when eaten, will give everlasting life to the king of all creation and, through him, to his entire kingdom. At first glance this comparison appears to be to the detriment of the Assyrian-Babylonian tree; indeed that was most likely its original intention.

But, truth be told, there is nothing to fear in the Assyrian-Babylonian conception. Christ's Life-giving Cross, of whose

Most Sacred Fruit the faithful partake in order to live, is likened in church hymns to the Tree of Life in Genesis, and there is a long tradition in church art that likens the theme of the cross to the theme of the Assyrian-Babylonian tree of life.

Let us examine another synthetic symbol of religion, this time related to the union of humans and animals. In its simplest form, this involves deities combining animal and human parts, with the dominance of the one or the other.

There are many Egyptian drawings of this sort. In more profound syntheses it is difficult or even impossible to determine which is the dominant element. The Sphinx, the Chimera, and so on are vivid examples of such symbols. The most impressive synthesis can be found in the Assyrian winged lions or bulls, whose colossal statues were placed as defenders at the entrances to the palaces of Assyrian kings. These are figures in which human wisdom is combined with the soaring and rapid flight of the eagle and the strength of the lion or bull. Sometimes winged spirits with eagle heads guard the sacred tree or bless the king. It is clear that these guardians of the threshold are transcendent in relation to our world and therefore can only be represented symbolically.

The cherubim, i.e., the "living beings," *to zoa*, supporting the throne of God's Glory in the vision of the prophet Ezekiel (Ez. 1:10; cf. Rev. 4:6–8) and represented on the ark of the covenant, on the *miskan*, and on the *parochet* of the Old Testament Temple can be likened, in their external form, to the Assyrian defender-spirits. "The cherubim had the form of winged beings, expressing human reason, strength of will, the courage of a lion, and the soaring flight of an eagle."[7]

"They are winged animals, not resembling any actual animals." The tetramorph of Christian iconography, combining

7. I. Troitsky, *Biblical Archeology*, St. Petersburg, 1913, 353 ff.

four creatures, man, lion, bull, and eagle, and symbolizing the four Evangelists (in particular, on church vaults), represents different symbolic images of the same spiritual being, or even the symbols of the Evangelists; these basic physiological and ontological types of the human being must be viewed not separately but as one whole. Meanwhile, the cherubim of the Old Testament became an object of diligent and profound study among the Kabbalists.

We will conclude our discussion of such synthetic symbols by asking the question: Are they merely the products of religious speculation or are they real visions of the spirit soaring to heavenly heights?

The answer must be that they are real visions. Prophetic visions are concrete perceptions, not abstract theological speculations. What Ezekiel saw is unimaginable to us not because it is too difficult for us to understand, but because it is beyond anything we have experienced. Our ability to see what the Prophet saw is not just poor; it is non-existent. However, the experience of synthetic vision is repeated each time the spiritual gaze acquires the power to soar above the sensuous, "fleshly" world.

Synthetic visions of an individual's integral life are possible, as are synthetic visions of the life of nations and states. The spiritual gaze can capture in a single focus entire epochs of world history and even the whole universe. As an example of this let us mention a vision of St. Benedict as recounted by St. Gregory: In the dead of night Benedict suddenly beheld a flood of light shining down from above more brilliant than the sun, and with it every trace of darkness cleared away. According to his own description, the whole world was gathered up before his eyes "in what appeared to be a single ray of light."[8]

8. *S. Gregorii Magni Operum*, Tome III, 1615.

That is the life of the world as it is seen in its integral oneness; and the higher life, living life, or spirituality perceived concretely as light—this higher life is revealed to the open eyes in integral forms. That is how the Church was revealed to St. Hermas, who saw this catholic being as a light-suffused Tower and as a Woman full of splendor. Another content of the Church, one that highlights the importance of personal experience, is indicated by the 14th-century Archbishop of Salonika, Nicholas Kabasilas, an authoritative interpreter of the sacraments. Known not only as a profound theologian but also as one who livingly experienced the truth of the dogmas, he provided very important guidance regarding how one should understand the unity of the Church.

He writes: "The role of the sacrament of communion in the Church is not a symbolic one, but can be likened to the role of the heart in the body, the role of the roots of a tree, or (as the Lord said) the role of the vine with respect to the grapes; for what we have here is not similarity of name, but true identity, since the sacrament is the body and blood of Christ. If one could see Christ's Church exactly in the form in which she is united with Christ and participates in His flesh, he would see her as the body of the Lord and nothing else. Paul writes: 'Now ye are the body of Christ, and members in particular' (1 Cor. 1:27)."[9]

9. Nicholas Kabasilas, *Explanation of the Divine Liturgy*, Russ. trans., chap. 38, St. Petersburg, 1857.

12

The Meaning of Genus

IF LIFE, EVEN IN ITS EXTERNAL FORM when it is perceived in a painting or in a piece of sculpture, is *mia dia pollen,* a *universale,* then are not living organisms, these internally formed sculptures of life, even more super-singular? In fact, living, animate matter, hylozoism and hylopsychism, was the starting point of ancient philosophy. Wonder—which according to both Plato and Aristotle constitutes the origin and driving force of philosophy—was first prompted by the contradictory combination of oneness and multiplicity in life. Thus, the problem of *hen kai polla* stretched like a scarlet thread from the beginning to the end of ancient philosophy. The term "genus"—this most essential term in the study of life—turned out to be foundational in the development of idealism. And it is not by accident that logic, that offspring of idealism, has made use of a term that has biological and social connotations.

In our modern understanding a genus is a collection, an ensemble, an aggregate, a logical quantity, i.e., an external and mechanical unity, nothing more. But in the ancient world it meant essential oneness, the one object of knowledge.

The sensitivity of our vision to what is individual verges on sickness, as does, and even more so, the sensitivity to it of our feeling of life and understanding of life. Individualism, i.e., nominalism, is the sickness of our time. It was only through great exertion that ancient man could see what was isolated and individual; and only sinning could produce in him a sensation of the latter. He viewed individualism as an act of deliberate separation, splitting off, and he considered it a fault, *adikia*, an injustice, as Anaximander called it.[1]

According to this same thinker,[2] those who sinned in this way were subject to a fateful retribution, *dike*, consisting of the dissolution or annihilation of the individual. Ancient man saw reality not as a series of separate points, and not as a chaos where all demarcations were erased; he saw it as an organism. Only a great exertion of the consciousness could make it possible to see the individual organs in their isolation. Everyday consciousness, however, views them as one. Genus is what binds together this mysterious oneness. This realization of *hen kai polla* is what was meant by genus in its ancient sense. The separateness of genus is only apparent and momentary. If we, people of the 20th century who have almost totally lost the vision of oneness, who for a long time have not been able to see the forest for the trees, if we are to see this oneness of genus once again, we will have to overcome this shortcoming of our vision by using the power of our thought. This can be done by using the following hypotheses: four-dimensional vision, the oneness of blood or the oneness of seed, the oneness of biological shape, and purely mystical oneness.

We should keep in mind, though, that these hypotheses are nothing more than crutches by which we try to overcome our deficiencies. The Greeks *saw hen kai polla,* and this vision was the basis of their philosophy and made the latter an enterprise full of vital interest and excitement. We however have to convince ourselves first of all of the existence not only of *polla* but also of *hen*—of the existence of *hen kai polla,* and only then, having con-

1. Theophrasti Physic, opinionum, fr. 2.
2. Ibid.

structed for ourselves the fundamental problem of philosophy, can we began to philosophize, i.e., to solve this problem. For us philosophy has become something like an intellectual exercise; for the Greeks it was not an external decoration of life but the inner beauty of the latter and an elucidation of its psychophysical and social structure.

13

Genus and Species

LET US LOOK MORE CLOSELY at the original meaning of the words
"genus" and "species." Having peeled off the juridical and philosophical layers from these words, let us enter into the recesses of
their primary kernel, as if we were entering a cave or a creative
womb of being; and having entered, let us try to make a home for
ourselves in the primordial darkness surrounding us.

We sometimes say that among a group of people there is a
"family resemblance," that they have "something in common."
But what is this common thing? Isidore, Bishop of Seville, says
"*gens ab uno principio est multitudo orta*" (genus is a multiplicity
begotten by one principle).[1]

The word *gens*, just as words with the same root (the Latin
genus and the Greeek *genos*), involves the notion of birth. We
find this in writers of the 7th and 9th centuries. "*Gens appellata
propter generationes, id est gignendo, sicut natio a nascendo* (genus
is derived from *genarationes*, i.e., birth-giving, just as nation is
derived from the same thing)"[2] declares the above-mentioned
saint. His explanation is also applicable, *mutatis mutandis*, to the
Russian *rod* (kind or race) and *narod* (nation), both derived from

---

1. S. Isidori Hispalensis, *Episcopi Etymologiarium*, cap. 2.
2. Ibid.

rozhdat (to give birth). We find the same explanation in Alcuin (735–803), born a century after Isidore. In Alcuin's *Disputatio puerorum*, the boys carry on the following dialogue:

Question: *Quid est genus?* (What is genus?)

Answer: *Genus est a gignendo dictum, an derivativum nomen a terra, ex qua omnium gignuntur.* (Genus is derived from to give birth or from the earth out of which all things are born.)

Question: *Quomodo?* (In what manner?)

Answer: *Ge enim graece terra dicitur.* (In Greek, *gen* means earth.)[3]

The transition from the Latin *genus* to the Greek *ge* is an example of etymological naivete, but nevertheless it is a beautiful one, for it contains the profound idea that the Earth is the mother of all things.

Related to this cluster of words are the Sanskrit *ja, janati,* and *jajanmi* (to give birth, to generate); *jaje* (I am born); *janas* (entity, essence); *janus* (gender); *janita, janitar* (*genitor,* birth-giver); *janitri* (*genetrix,* birth-mother); *jatis* (birth). Also related to this are the Vedic *gna* or the more colloquial *jani* (woman); the Zend *zan* (to give birth), *ghena* (woman); the Greek *gignomai, geneter, geneteira, genesis, gyne* and so on; the Latin *gigno, genui, genitor, genetrix, gnascor, genor, genius, natura,* and so on; the Gothic *kuni*; and the Russian *zhena, zhenshchina* (woman).[4]

Thus, etymology confirms that it is birth that makes a genus a genus. Members of the same genus (relatives) bear the same name. What they have in common is not abstractly common but concretely common; it is *one* in them. This is their genus. Their genus is numerically identical in them. The common traits are

3. B.F. Albini seu Alcuini, *Operum* pars VIII.

4. This etymological section is indebted to the linguists A.Walde, E. Boisac, G. Curtius and W. Prellwitz.—Trans.

not what makes them members of the same genus; rather, the fact that they are members of the same genus is what produces the common traits.

So, when the fact of belonging to the same genus (kinship) is conceived concretely, it becomes the same thing as genus itself. The common traits are due to the oneness of the genus; this one principle shines through them, and—what is most remarkable—it shines forth not in one or another limited association of traits, but in their all, everywhere in them, always in them; their all is, in essence, one; after careful examination it turns out to be one. This one in them is genus, while the one that shines through their all, this one is the energy of the genus, or the genus in terms of its energy. Since they are born of the same root, kin are one—they are genus, *genos*, *gens*-genus.

Genus shines everywhere through everything, but nowhere is it accessible to our senses. Everything bears the stamp of genus, but any attempt to show exactly where it resides is an exercise in futility. Let us try to clarify this by a plainer example—the experience we have of our personhood. Where does it reside? For our sense experience—nowhere. Not in our hands, not in our feet, not in our head, not in our voice, not in our gait, not in our bearing, etc. In short, it resides in nothing that we can see, hear, touch, or smell. Nevertheless, everyone knows that personhood is visible in face, hands, gait, and bearing; that it is audible in the intonation and timbre of our voice.

Our personhood is seen, heard, felt, and smelled when behind eye, ear, hand, and nose there operate *another* eye, ear, hand, and nose. Human personhood, not given to us through sense perception, everywhere shining through sensuous material, always glimmering between sensuous material as if hidden behind a picket fence—personhood is *ens realior* compared with the sensuous shell in which it is apprehended; personhood is higher-density reality compared with the thin-gruel reality of the sensuous.

[71]

As the fog of sensuousness is dissipated in our consciousness, the more clearly we perceive the more essential lineaments of the inner human being. For example, Stephen the Sabait had the ability to "see with the spirit." He affirmed: "God has endowed me with the gift of seeing and hearing the thoughts and secret passions of people we see, people we hear about, people we encounter; and thus I have knowledge of all their psychic and spiritual deficiencies."[5] Elsewhere he says: "Nothing of your manner of life is hidden from me; and if I wanted to list all your secrets, I could do so with God's aid."[6]

The same thing goes for genus. Among members of the same genus (kin) it is impossible to find a link or (among the individuals) a trait that one could relate to genus. There is no member of the genus about whom it could be said: "this is the genus."

There's more. Genus is generated from one root, from "one principle, *unius principii*," according to St. Isidore;[7] but one cannot say that this one root or principle is the genus. The root is the root and the branches are the branches; and the root in the branches is not more than they themselves—in each other. The root is not in them, and they are not in each other and not in the root, but there is something that is one in them; and it is through this something that all of them are in each other and in the root, that the root is in them.

Birth binds kin into one whole; or more precisely, on the unseen genus it brings forth sprouts of unseen forms or persons of the kin, their "hypostases" (to use a patristic term). But, again, birth is a property not of the genus, but only of its members; that is, birth is something like the surface of genus, not it itself. Here is what St. John of Damascus says: "Birth, in relation to bodies,

5. Vita S. Stephani, *Acta Sanctorum*, Paris and Rome, 1867.
6. Ibid.
7. S. Isidori, ibid.

signifies the generation of a unisubstantial hypostasis from the union of male with female. From this we learn that to give birth is a property not of the nature but of the hypostasis, for if birth were a property of the nature, we would not see in the same nature the born and the not born."[8]

Thus, birth itself is not a property of genus, but only a hypostasis of the latter; but at the same time it is indisputable that in birth we are more conscious of the presence of genus than, say, in the fulfillment of our work responsibilities. There is some difference in the sensation of the noumenal seed of things when performing different activities and in the case of different properties of its hypostases.

Just as the personhood of an individual human being shines through with different degrees of expressiveness in his various actions, in his various states, properties, and organs, so in the case of a multiplicity of individuals (a genus) there are regions of greater or lesser transparence. And if we accept that it is easy to ascertain a person's spiritual state by reading his face, but that it is very difficult to do so by reading his spine, it should not surprise us that in a multiplicity of individuals the noumenal pulse rate is easy to read in some places, whereas in other places it can be determined only by means of highly sensitive and refined techniques.

That is why one can with some justice give symbolic names reflecting the noumenal world to these thin, transparent places of the phenomenal world. For example, we use the symbolic terms "blood" and "seed" to denote kinship (genus). By the way, the Latin word for "seed," *germen*, from *gen-men*, is derived from the same root as *gens-genus*.

But, again, flowing blood and ejected seed are only bearers of genus, not genus itself; they are only the channels through which

8. S. Ioannis Damasceni, *De fide orthodoxa*, lib. 4, cap. VII.

genus flows. Blood and seed are seen, whereas genus is unseen. Blood and seed are here or there, whereas genus is neither here nor there; it is both here and there. Blood and seed are or were or will be; genus is, was, and will be, all three. Genus is one, though it can shine forth everywhere with greater or lesser clarity. Though it appears in a multiplicity of things, genus only glimmers; it can only be felt, not touched.

Genus does not possess visual, tactile, olfactory, or auditory definiteness. Unstructured in appearance, blood and seed by their formlessness symbolize the sensuous formlessness of genus. Genus is invisible and unseen, and therefore is incorporeal as well. However, in the members of the genus, its birth-products, it becomes visible in the form of species, and there is a multiplicity of such forms.

In growing, members of a genus change—of course, not only in the quantitative but also in the qualitative sense. A 7-pound infant grows into a 170-pound man; there are changes in the color of hair, face, and even hands; in the strength of muscles and bones; in tastes, manners, knowledge, habits, and even character. It seems there is no trait or combination of traits about which it could be said without hesitation: "this is an invariant."[9] Nevertheless, the person remains identical to himself, not only because of his consciousness of self but also because of something apprehended from outside.

9. The theory of invariants, one of the most significant achievements of mathematical analysis in the second half of the 19th century, is little used in philosophy and awaits its interpreter. The notion of invariants and the kindred covariant, concomitant, simultant, resultant, discriminant, and so on are destined, in the future, to impart a mighty impulse to the general understanding of life. One feels that philosophy is already groping toward these formal theories of mathematics. Here, it is likely that the largest fruits will be brought forth by that version of the theory of invariants that is called "symbolic" and is obscurely drawn toward the general principles of thought. In the domain of nature-philosophy, the applicability of the theory of invariants to the principle of relativity has already been shown. Thus, the

Genus and Species

A human being's personhood, despite all its changes, unchangeably shines forth in his face. In the face there is something unseen that is more definite than everything that is seen—a kind of invariant, to use a mathematical term.

Not determined by the enumeration of traits, not unlike a ray of light slipping away from the knife of analysis, personhood is something that abides in the face; the rushing cyclone of Time blows away all empirical unchangeability, but personhood, like a guiding star, remains constant.

Also, think of a rainbow woven of the purest rays which remains unshaken by a hurricane that uproots the largest trees and tears to shreds the swirling clouds with its crazy wind. Every particular state of a human being, every moment of his growth, every movement of his, weak or strong, shines forth with the rays of his personhood, his "species." These species are in the genus; they abide in it, participate in it, partake of it; or, if you will, genus is present in them. But, most concisely: the species of a genus are in the genus. A genus and its species are essences from which the genus itself is speciesless, but contains species, and shines forth with its species in the members of the genus.

This shining forth defines the significance of genus members for eternity. The member is defined by the genus, becomes capable of progeny, *gennaios*; the member is defined by his "breeding"; it is said he is "well bred," of "noble birth." This means that genus clearly shines forth from him. Indeed, what is noble birth if not the transparence of the empirical shell for empirical content? "Apples of gold in transparent vessels of silver" (Prov. 25:11)—is this not said about noble birth? For of noble

end of the 19th century and the beginning of the 20th century are marked by a syn-. cretism of domains which seem foreign to one another, i.e., the theory of forms and the theory of invariants, non-Euclidean and multidimensional geometries, projective geometry and group theory, set theory, the electromagnetic theory of light, relativity, electron theory, etc.

birth is he whose species is well-defined, whole, untroubled, clearly etched. Of noble birth is he in whose species is seen his genus, i.e., in whose face is seen the eternal and universal.

Derivative layers are deposited on the basic meaning of the word *genos*. In Homer, *genos* means: (1) root, origin, genus, or stirps; (2) the place of someone's origin; (3) continuation of a genus, *gentis propago*; (4) people of the same age or generation; (5) age—the expression *genei* is equivalent to *aetate*, *natu*; (6) abstractly, a category or class (e.g., *hemitheon genos andron*). The last is encountered mainly in the Homeric hymns; that is, this sense is more ancient than the others.

Later writers emphasize the aspect of abstract multiplicity in the word *genos*. *Genos* begins to mean nation, *natio*, or clan, *gens*, *ethnos*; literary genre; gender; people in general, the human race; and finally (in Aelianus, Philostratus, and others) a collective; and here it is combined with the plural number. This replacement, in the content of the word *genos*, of real unity by collective unity was marked by the establishment in philosophy of the word *classis*, i.e., by a word denoting external unity, imposed by command or juridical decree and having no relation to inner unity or unity by birth.

In the guise of "class,"[10] genus (or *genos*) entered into the very heart of western European philosophy and became the embryo of the future nominalism. From the very beginning, western European thought was destined to follow the path of nominal-

---

10. Western philosophy is marked by the tendency to replace the term "genus" with the term "class," and at present the latter is used almost exclusively, especially by British thinkers. If western philosophy completely lacked terms of the form *genos* and *genus*, such a replacement would be understandable and would be nothing more than an error of confusion. But it is impossible not to see an impoverishment of thought in what seems a conscious replacement of the Greek *genos* first by the Latin *genus* instead of *gens* and then by the term *classis*. Thus, life processes are replaced by a mechanical process, motherhood by an incubator, family by a

ism, for this negation of real unity (the replacement of genus by class) was grafted to the very roots of this thought. It was only a question of time before this nominalistic embryo grew and evolved, and later history has shown clearly the terrible consequences connected with this poor choice of fundamental terms.

contract, prayer by a deal, and statecraft by socialism. Despite the powerful ontology of the East, the West could not understand anything except the epiphenomena. Such it has been, and such it has remained. The replacement of genos by classis is sufficient to explain the inevitability of the schism between the West and the Church! But one can name hundreds of examples of such classis. The astonishing thing is not that schism has occurred, but that for some mysterious reason it has not been detected for such a long time.

A vivid example of such superficiality of western thought can be found in Hegel. This representative of idealism in the West declares without embarrassment that the word "idea" is not necessary, for it can be successfully replaced by the word "sort," "*Art.*"

14

Idea and Countenance

HOW CAN WE NOW UNDERSTAND that concrete generality, that contemplated *universale*, that clearly defined *hen kai polla* that lies at the basis of all knowledge? In attempting to approach such an understanding we always collided with the problem of life; and this problem became the problem of the human body. The latter in turn was concentrated in the problem of the face, and the mystery of the face became the problem of the spiritual countenance [*lik* in Russian]. But here we must inevitably ask ourselves: "Did the reduction of idealism to the study of the countenance come about by chance, depending on the artificial selection of explanatory examples, or is idealism rooted in a heightened attention to the countenance by the very nature of the matter?"

Recalling that ancient idealism had its origin in Socrates' discovery of man for philosophy and in the study of human nature, and then recalling that for antiquity in general and for Socrates in particular man was the Alpha and the Omega of life-understanding, and recalling the particular anthropocentricity of the ancient Greek worldview in the second period of the development of Greek philosophy, and, finally, focusing attention on the innate sensitivity of the ancient Greeks to the beauty of the human body—we will inevitably come to the insight that idealism is oriented toward the countenance (for it is by his countenance that a man is man), and that idea is connected with countenance much more intimately than with any one of the explanatory examples,

[79]

as can be understood from the preceding discussion. Yes, idea is the face of the face: it is countenance. This conclusion is quite probable, but it becomes a certainty if we take the trouble to analyze etymologically the word that has become fundamental in the language of idealism, i.e., the technical term *eidos* or *idea*.

What do the words *eidos* and *idea* mean? The Alexandrian lexicographer Hesychius, who lived five centuries after Christ, adduced the following synonyms of *eidos*: "*kaira*, heat, being red hot; *chroma*, color of skin or body; *soma*, body; *opsis*, sight, look of the face, vision; *prosopon*, face, countenance, person."[1] The word *idea*, however, is totally absent from his Glossary. In 891, the Patriarch Photius explains ideas through *morphos* and with reference to Plato's *Alcibiades*, where this word is produced *apo tou idesthai* (from "to be visible").[2] Meantime, the word *eidos* is in a lost passage of Photius's manuscripts, so that it remains unexplained. In 977, the *Sudae Lexicon* explains ideas as *tas theories* (contemplations). Further, it indicates that "*Idea ho Platon kai eidos oniomazei kai genos kai paradeigma kai archen kai aition—idea der logou ho charakter*" (With idea Plato denotes species, genus, example, principle, and cause; as a concept idea signifies distinctive character).[3] But besides a concrete meaning, *idea* also acquires the sense of an abstract class. Anthimos Gazis explains *eidos* through "*morphe, theoria, opsis tou prosopou. Blepsimpn, kittagma*" (shape, contemplation, facial features, species). He explains idea through "*eidos, morphe, blemma schema, hei phainomene morphe tou somatos e tou prosopou, theoria, Tropos, sunetheia, homoiuotes, hypothesis, kairos*" (species, shape, gaze, image, habit, simulacrum, presupposition, moment).

1. *Hesycii Dictionarium.*
2. *Photii Lexicon*, Lipsiae, 1808.
3. *Sudae Lexicon*, vol. I, 1854.

This is followed by the explanation of idea as a philosophical term.

The etymology of the words that interest us supports fully the later lexicographic explanations and deepens our understanding of these words, for the notion of seeing or vision merges here with the notion of knowledge. Here are words with the same root as *eidos*: the Sanskrit *vedah*, knowledge; the Lithuanian *veidas*, face; the Old Church Slavonic *VID*. At their basis lies the hypothetical form *ueides-*; cf. the Irish *fiand* (iae<ei)—front, *coram*, the Gallic *gwydd*, presence (<the Celtic *veido-s*). The root *veid*, to see, to know; cf. the Greek *idein, oida*.

Cf. also the Gothic *unweis*, ignoramus, *unwis*, the Norric *viss*, knowing, wise, *wisa*, knowledge, manner <*ueid(e)*. The Greek *idea*, external form, appearence, form has its origin in the hypothetical form *Fidesa*. Parallels of it are the Gothic *FisFos*, the Attic *isos*, equal, originating from the form *FitoFo* or *uids-uo*. Related to this are the Homeric *eidulis*, of beautiful appearance, *eidolon* (*-o/u/o-?), simulacrum, image, poetic alpha-[=]*eidelos* invisible, the Lithuanian *vaidalos*, appearance, and *pavidalas* from poetic *eiddulis, -idos*, knower, the Sanskrit *vidurah*, one who understands, is clever, the Lithuanian *pa-viduls*, envious, and *pa-vidulis*, portrait, the Prussian *pa-vudulis*, iris in the sense of popular, *chore pupille*, puppet, *"chelovechek"* (little man), the Gothic *faiirweitl*, spectacle, *phrontesin*, according to Hesychius, *idmon-onos*, learned in something, the Sanskit *vidman*, to know, wisdom, poetic, *idris = ios*, scholar, clever, the Norric *vitr*, genus, *vitrs*, clever, or the Attici *stor*—knower, *indalliomai*, to render visible, to appear, the Sanskrit *vindatim*, to find, etc.

So, what is an idea? It is a species, though not a species in and of itself, but a species as giving knowledge of that of which it is a species. An idea is the face of reality and, *par excellence*, the human face, though not in its empirical randomness but in its cognitive value; i.e., the human visage or countenance. "Eidos, idea means species, image. Plato appropriated this term, first of all, because the generality of things, in which together with Socrates he saw the sole object of true knowledge, is attained by us through the fusion of things, and things are usually fused according to species or image."[4] Thus, Plato says that "*ho men gar sunopyikos, ho de me ou;*"[5] as well as "*eis mian t'idean sunoronta agein ta pollokei diesparmena*" (one capable of surveying all things together is a dialectician; a contemplator focuses all scattered things into one idea).[6]

However, in this linkage in idea of knowledge and vision there is something far deeper than an "ordinary" connection. "Sensations," declares E. Laas, "differ according to their quality. Theoretically, the most valuable of the senses is sight. Plato, too, has a high opinion of sight."[7]

Plato sings the praises of sight and light: "As far as beauty is concerned, it shone—*elampen*—while still there, and when it came here, we noticed the vividness of its radiance by the clearest of our senses. For among the bodily senses, sight is considered to be the most acute. This character (the accessibility to sense perception) is possessed by beauty alone; it alone is destined to be the clearest and most pleasing. When an initiate, contemplating much that is over there, looks at a divinelike face, with the imprint of great beauty, or when he looks at a beautiful body, he begins to tremble and is embraced by fear of what is over there, but when he looks more closely, he treats this thing as if it were a god and, if not for his fear he would be like one in ecstasy and would bring sacrifices to this thing of beauty as to a sacred sculpture or god; this vision of beauty produces a change in him through fear, throwing him into a sweat and making an extraor-

4. A. Giliarov, *Plato as a Historical Witness*, Kiev, 1891, 123, 228 note.
5. *Republic* 531d.
6. *Phaedrus* 265d.
7. E. Laas, *Idealismus und Positivismus*, 36.

dinary warmth flow through his body. Receiving through the organ of sight the radiation of the beautiful, he becomes warm."[8]

"Do you understand," exclaims Plato in another passage,[9] "what a precious power of seeing and being seen the Maker of the senses has created?" And then he declares that the advantage of seeing over the other senses consists in the fact that sound and hearing do not require a medium, whereas light is needed for the visible and vision. Finally, in yet another passage where he describes the advantages of vision, he indicates the dispassion of the latter: "All active things are seen easily and vividly without producing sorrow or pleasure, which for example are impressions of that vision about which we said previously that its form in the daytime is a connected body. For the organ of vision does not experience pain from cutting, burning, or other things just as it does not receive pleasure from them if it returns to its previous state."[10]

This comprises Plato's direct testimony. But even if this testimony did not exist, it would not be difficult to guess its content. For Greek thought is entirely grounded upon the fundamental perception of light, and Greek psychology is completely suffused with categories of visual impressions. It is clear that the supreme principle of knowledge and being—idea—can in concrete experience be connected only with seeing and the seen.[11]

Let us now consider the semasiology of the words that interest us.

In Homer, the word *eidos* is encountered at least 66 times, 19 times in the *Iliad*, 30 times in the *Odyssey*, and in six of the 33 hymns for a total of 17 times. Let us note that the *Iliad* contains

8. *Phaedrus* 250d–251a.

9. *Republic* VI.

10. *Timaeus* 64d,r

11. On light as the supreme principle of knowledge and beauty, see P. Florensky, *The Pillar and Ground of the Truth*, 53–79.

about 15,700 lines, the *Odyssey* about 17,500 lines, and the hymns about 2,416 lines.

In other words, in the *Odyssey* the word *eidos* occurs more than 1.5 times more frequently than in the *Iliad*, and almost six times more frequently than in the hymns.

These are some of the moments in the history of the words *eidos* and *idea*. But somehow they do not satisfy. A careful student of Plato cannot fail to come away with the impression that the philosopher is speaking of certain religious values, and that the enigmatic appearance in philosophy of the words *eidos* and *idea* has a long underground history, hidden in the sanctuaries of mystical cults. This history has not yet been fully studied.

We find very important guidance on this matter in the Dictionary of Julius Pollux. Pollux lists the synonymic names of the gods and various higher beings. Then he names the different parts of a temple. Finally, he describes the entities before which the service is celebrated: sculptures, statues, wooden statues, seats of the gods, images of gods, icons, simulacra, figures, species, forms are what we venerate.[12]

Then there is a discussion of sacrificial altars.

Divine images, and preeminently those connected with mysteries, were called *eide* and *ideai*. Let us indicate how many other Platonic terms are contained in this passage of Pollux. To be sure, Plato also uses *eidos* and *idea* as general names for concrete, contemplated beauty. Such is a remarkable passage from Pollux. I discovered this passage on October 26, 1914, after many futile searches of different authors, though I never lost the certainty that such a passage must exist somewhere. Thankfully, my premonition was justified.

Euripides' "Bacchae" speaks of what is inaccessible to the non-initiate. But precisely what is inaccessible? The general organiza-

---

12. *Julii Pollucis Onomasticon*, Berlin, 1846, I, 3.

tion of orgies and their form was familiar to everyone, and is described in this tragedy by Dionysus himself. So, it is a question not of species but of the vision seen by the bacchantes themselves, i.e., of Dionysus himself and of the transfigured countenance of all reality, perhaps of some image of Dionysus.

How should we understand the meaning of the *eideai* and *eide* of which Pollux speaks? On my part, I assume that these are not images of gods but the very countenances of gods and demons appearing in the mysteries to initiates. Here we have gained entry into the holy of holies of Plato's philosophy, where *eidos* and *idea* become concrete and full of life as well as transcendent. The enigmatic kernel of Platonism is mystery; for the goal of initiation was identical to the goal of philosophy: to develop the capacity for mystical contemplation and directly to see *mistika theamata* (mystical visions).

The sacred apparitions that passed before the eyes of the ecstatic contemplator of the other world—these are Plato's heavenly countenances or supra-sensuous ideas. Let us draw attention to the fact that *eidolon* is the diminutive of *eidos* and means the same thing as *eidos* or *idea*. There is no disputing the truth of Plutarch's assertion that the mysteries "provide the best explanation of the nature of demons."[13]

This seems to be the most probable origin of Plato's philosophy. If that is indeed the case, this makes it possible to understand Plato's words in the *Phaedrus* to the effect that one who loves is ready to bring sacrifices to the beloved as *"agalmaii kai theoi"* (as to a statue and god). For *eros* shows an idea in the beloved's face, and the word idea is, according to Pollux, synonymous with *agalma*. Consequently, the one who loves sees a divine counte-

---

13. K. de Jorg, *Das antike Mysterienwesen in Religionsgeschichte, ethnologischer und pschycologischer Bedeutung*, Leiden, 1909.

nance in the beloved's face and desires to make an appropriate offering to it. That is Plato's thought.

But did something really appear in the mysteries that only the initiated could grasp? Without inquiring in detail into this complex problem, we will consider only one example, which confirms this belief of the ancients. Pausanius tells of a temple of Isis near Delphi. According to the pious traveler, this was the "holiest of all the temples built by the Greeks to honor the Egyptian goddess."[14] Mysteries were enacted in this temple. They say that an uninitiated man who did not have the right to enter the temple did in fact out of curiosity enter it when the sacred flame was burning there. But when he returned home and told what he had seen, he gave up the soul.[15] Small countenances of the heavenly foundations of life—that is what ideas are.

14. *Pausaniae Graeciae Descriptio*, 1829, 350.
15. Alpha Omega. Gemma Magica.

15

The Fundamental Aspirations of Idealism

GRADUALLY PENETRATING deeper and deeper into life, we have carved out a series of steps leading to an understanding of the fundamental aspirations of idealism. You might object, however, that we are considering only the simulacra of immanent—Aristotelean—ideas but are very far from approaching transcendent Platonic ideas.

But is that really the case? Is what we are saying only immanent in nature? Is there no transcendence here?

But can one speak of something that is partly immanent and partly transcendent?

But is it possible to have something that is totally transcendent or totally immanent?

Why not?

Because the transcendent and the immanent are both relative. The immanent is immanent in relation to something, and the transcendent is transcendent in relation to something. That which is transcendent to one thing can be immanent to another thing.

Is it impossible to imagine the transcendent without any relation to something?

Yes, I think it is impossible. The very act of talking about the transcendent makes it immanent in some sense.

What about the immanent?

Same thing. It's impossible to talk about the purely immanent, for one can talk only about what in some sense goes beyond the talker, is separated from and opposed to him, transcends him.

You're saying one can't talk about the transcendent because it's not immanent, and one can't talk about the immanent because it's not transcendent.

That's exactly right. If we talk about something, it must be both transcendent and immanent.

But this is on the cognitive plane. Our discussion began with ontology. Where is the transcendent moment of a work of art, for example?

Perhaps in the fact that an artist's intention that is embodied in one material can also be embodied in another material. Thus, it is not absolutely connected with the material in which it is embodied. In the same way, a human countenance is embodied in a particular face even though the material of the latter is in a state of constant flux. Here, the connection between a countenance and the material in which it is embodied is even less absolute. Thus, in the series of our approaches to an understanding of idealism, the transcendent moment of the idea tends to increase.

One can even go further. One can, for example, examine the effect of a work of art on individuals and on society. In creating a body for some spiritual principle, an artist or poet no longer has the power to interrupt the flow of energy streaming from a new center. This new center forms persons created in its image and drawn into its sphere of influence. The epidemic of suicides emanating from "Werther," the "Weltschmerz" having its origin in "Faust," the demonism rooted in the poems of Byron, and suchlike mass effects, had their source not in Goethe or Byron, but in Werther, Faust, the Corsair, and Cain, who burst through the door opened for them by their poets and then, as transcendent entities, made a home for themselves in men's souls. But before their embodiment and after it, Werther, Faust, Onegin, and oth-

[88]

ers continue to exist independently of those in whom they are embodied as well as those who created them. *Idées-forces,* a term coined by Fouillée, represent such a high degree of transcendence that they can almost be regarded as autonomous entities. Those statues and paintings which in ancient Greece surrounded pregnant women so that the child who was carried would be subjected to the influence of these works of art—can they not, in relation to the child, be viewed as ideas and in fact as transcendent ideas? Is there a very great distance between such idealism and strict realism?

But one can go even further, creating a greater separation of the energy of the idea from the idea itself.

16

Genesis, Genitura, and *Gandhara*

NOTHING EXTERNAL, in and of itself, can be identified with the *universale*, but on the other hand the all, in one way or another, is transilluminated by it. From this, with necessity, is born the notion of the correspondence of different external realms that are internally identical. All things correspond; all things breathe harmoniously; *panta sumpnoia*. But in those places where the rough crust is illuminated and where matter is most compliant under the fingers "light as a dream" of the Artist who molds it—in those places the correspondences must seek more highly saturated and reciprocal responses—purer echoes. In the fiery ether of the celestial spheres, where one finds "harmonious choirs of starry orbs," there thought has sought special signs concerning terrestrial events. A fundamental principle of the ancient worldview was the sympathy between the terrestrial and the celestial.

The premise of astrology is sympathy between the terrestrial and the celestial, and changes of the terrestrial in conformity with the influence of the celestial. Repeated in countless variants, this basic theme is characterized by many variegated nuances and degrees of clarity. But perhaps its most radical expression is the use in astrology of biological terms to describe the celestial sphere. I have in mind the terms *genesis* and *genitura*.

What are *genesis* and *genitura*? They are synonymous with

[91]

sperma and *semen*. It is true that Aristotle and then Galen and others introduced into the meaning of these terms certain differentiating nuances, but the latter were not significant enough to nullify their fundamental synonymity; moreover, later biology in the person of Isbrandi de Diemerbrock tended to reject totally the necessity of the earlier distinction. Therefore, the terms *genesis* and *genitura* can be conveyed through the word "seed." But the thought slumbering in the word "seed" is emphatically unfurled in the term *genitura*: being a future participle, *genitura* indicates the potentiality of that which is to be born from it; *genitura* is the present of some future. It is the face of some life, but in a sacred and empirically amorphous bud. However, the entire fullness of its definitions is already prefigured in this embryo of life; here, if you will, the ancient distinctions between *sperma* and *genesis* receive their meaning and place. Of course, a seed is *genitura* only when it is capable of fructifying, when it is alive, but this requires coupling with the feminine principle. If one sees in the animal world predominantly an expression of life, *genitura* must then refer predominantly to the animal seed.

But so far we have made only preliminary comments. The crux of the matter lies in the fact that, apart from their biological sense, the terms *genesis* and *genitura* have also acquired an astrological one. The same prefiguration of the person that with invisible lines is inscribed in a semen droplet is also inscribed in letters of stellar rays on the "fiery wall of the universe." Out of the etheric rays—or *aporroiai* or *influentiae*, influences or influxes—is woven in the maternal womb the tiny body of "the man who cometh into the world"; and not the semen droplet but an invisible noumenal force acting in this droplet is the true *genitura*. Why not transpose the name *genitura* from this droplet to the fire-inscribed celestial letters? And that's exactly what happened. The species or map of the sky at the moment of one's birth or—according to other systems of thought—at the moment of one's conception, was called the "theme of the *genitura*"—*thema* or *diathema tes geneseos*, as well as constellation, the abbreviated name of the "theme of *genitura*," or simply *genitura* or *genesis*. But since in astrology not the whole sky is operative, but only the zodiacal band of it, it must naturally follow that *genitura* is the name given to the zodiacal band of the celestial sphere under the aforementioned conditions—that is to say, it is like an instant photograph of the zodiacal part of the sky at the above-indicated moment of time. Let us note that the *genitura* is often called a horoscope. But this is incorrect, because this term actually refers to one of the four special points of the *genitura* called centers (*kentra*) in astrology: i.e., *to proskopon, to mesouranema, to dunon, to upogaion,* or *antimesouranema,* or *mesouranema.* Specifically, the horoscope is the ascending point of the *genitura.*

So, "a star's living light" is the seed, the species or idea transposed from earth to the sky. An idea is a "seed of the elements," "a spiritual star." Such is idealism as refracted in nature-philosophy. "The first thing one should know," says one of the nature-philosophers, "is that the external seed is not the true seed, as simple people think, but only the temple of the true seed, which is invisible, for if it dies, it will not bear any fruit; just as the external seed of animals is only the temple of the true seed. Philosophers give different names to these invisible spiritual seeds: constellations (because of their motion), seed reasons [*nous spermatikos*], roots of pure fruits, images or forms (because of their signature or sign), representations or ideas (because of the personal properties of the genus to be inscribed in the body), and solar dust particles (because of their inseparable velocity and uncountable set). The description is as follows: seeds are spiritual stars or constellations implanted in the element from God Himself in the first creation, watered by a living force of thoughtful art, and then, through natural bodies, projected into the theater of this world."[1] In the opinion of the cited author, this "living light" radiates from higher beings into lower ones. "For in it," he says, "is contained the Golden Chain of Homeric Celestial Wisdom, Jacob's Ladder, and the circular motion around nature when from God, as the first source, the river of goodness flows into the Angels, from the Angels into stars or constellations, and from stars into the heart and center of nature for the begetting of the universal seed in the elements, from the elements into the natural bodies of animals, earthly plants, and ores, and from these bodies into the microcosm which is man."[2]

The thoughts expressed here are not the product of any single thinker. They surface in many different combinations over the entire course of history, both ancient and modern. In Antiquity they are gathered into a single focus in the eclectic teaching of Plutarch. Like the majority of his contemporaries, Plutarch saw deities in celestial bodies; these were imperishable "logoi, emanations and species" of Divinity—"simulacra of gods."[3] According to his teaching, "in the heavens, in the super-lunar region, in stars, one sees the shining of imperishable embodiments of species, ideas, or logoi; in contrast, those ideas, logoi, emanations, seeds, simulacra, or impressions which are scattered in changeable entities in the earth, sea, plants, and animals—these things decay, disappear, are buried, and rise again into life, are reborn in new births."[4]

Thus, thrown into the sky, an idea does not remain there as an impersonal force, as a mere metaphysical principle. In idealistic conceptions, a celestial *genitura* takes on not only a philosophical persona but also one of popular thought, sometimes barely

1. Alpha Omega.
2. Ibid.
3. Plutarchus, *De Iside et Oside*, 36.
4. Ibid., 64.

sketched out, but sometimes clear and distinct. The doctrine of hypostatic ideas can, it seems, be encountered in every religion.

Among such doctrines we can list *gandhara*, which is clearly reminiscent of Leibniz's doctrine of the death-experiencing central part of an organism.

What is *gandhara?* Hildebrandt first of all regarded *gandhara* as the "genius of birth-giving,"[5] and later "as a participant in the conception of a spiritual entity originating from a previous being."[6] Oldenberg gives a similar definition: "das Lebenswesen" [living being] or "Wesenkeim" [kernal of being].[7] Conception, according to the Buddhist view, takes place from "the combination of three factors," from the "union of three: the father, the mother, and *gandhara*, or from "the coupling of the parents and the union of *gandhara* with the mother." This mysterious "embryo of life" of the Hindus is viewed as a forming power endowed with desire and will and also independent of the body it forms. This is quite similar to the Roman doctrine of geniuses, though among the Romans the ideal personal nature of geniuses is described much more clearly.

The modern understanding of genius makes it an immanent faculty of a person. However, for the Romans, genius or the feminine *junius* was an ideal principle and even a heavenly entity, emblematic of the earthly and being the patron of a person, place, phenomenon, or thing. Servius, a teacher of grammar and rhetoric who lived in the 4th century AD, defined genius as follows: "for the ancients, genius was a deity belonging to every place, man, or thing."

The basic meaning of the word genius indicates the notion of birth connected with the notion of life. According to the 8th-cen-

5. *Vedische Mythologie*, I, 427.
6. *Zur Bedeutung von Gandharva*, Breslau, 1906.
7. *Religion der Veda*, 249.

tury historian Paul the Deacon, *"genium appellant deum, qui vim obtineret rerum omnium generandarum"* (genius is the name given to god who possesses the power to beget all things). Initially, according to Kubler, the genius is a personification of birth-giving power. Genius is the true father of the members of a genus, for they obtain their life not as life in general but as the life of the genus, as the fullness of species, though they actualize not all the species contained in the genus, but each only its own. Genius as reality, as a higher reality, protecting the life of its members, is viewed as the ideal person of a given general life, as a given seed reality, as Genius. Genius is genus in its highest aspect. But it is also the countenance of a given person. In its first meaning, with predominance of the elemental moment, genius has some connection with Hebrew tetragrams and Hindu pitrams; in its second meaning, which emphasizes the formal and normative aspect of genius, it is closely related to hypostatic names, the doctrine of which we find not only in Rome but in all religions. Related to this are a number of Scandinavian gods who are present at a man's birth and serve as his patrons. Finally, the idea-angels of Philo and the Gnostics, the idea-deities of the Neoplatonists, and other similar entities are occult doctrines—branches from one and the same root.

To different degrees separated from and introduced into the empirical realm, *universalia*, in proportion to their embodiment, raise new questions—regarding the idea of ideas, for in relation to one another they turn out to be singularities, demanding a higher principle above themselves. The doctrine of the hierarchy of heavenly essences arises, and the whole pyramid of ideas ascends to its apex—to the idea of ideas, *"idea ton ideon"* (as Philo called it), to God, the Essence of all essences, for only in Him do they obtain their reason and their reality. Here arises the question of the self-grounding of God, and the conception of idealism inevitably becomes a problem of theodicy. When investigating the latter it turned out that, in the proper and ultimate sense, only Triunity is *hen kai polla*, i.e., only in Triunity is the fundamental requirement of all philosophy fulfilled. In addition, in the dogma of Trinity the fundamental themes of idealism, heard separately and preliminarily among different thinkers, are intertwined into one and sound forth with extreme clarity. Birth, life, beauty, creativity, unity in diversity, knowing love, eternity, and so on—are these particular aspects of the dogma of Trinity not, in a faint glimmer, objects of vivid interest for all idealism? That is why the supreme dogma of faith is that watershed from which philosophical reflections flow in different directions. Ivan Kireevsky wrote the following to A.I. Koshelev on October 2, 1852: "The doctrine of the Holy Trinity attracts my mind not only because it is the supreme center of the sacred truths communicated to us by Revelation, but also because, engaged on a work of philosophy, I came to the conclusion that the direction of philosophy depends, in its first principle, on the idea we have of the Holy Trinity."[8]

8. N. Elagin, *Materials for a Biography of I. V. Kireevsky,* Moscow, 1912, vol. 1, 74.